TEACH YOURSELF BOOKS

CANOEING

A PRACTICAL INTRODUCTION TO CANOEING AND KAYAKING

NTC Publishing Group

TEACH YOURSELF BOOKS

CANOEING

A PRACTICAL INTRODUCTION TO CANOEING AND KAYAKING

Ray Rowe

NTC Publishing Group

Log-renowned as *the* authoritative source for self-guided
learning – with more than 30 million copies sold worldwide –
the *Teach Yourself* series includes over 200 titles in the fields
of languages, crafts, hobbies, sports, and other leisure activities.

This edition was first published in 1993 by NTC Publishing
Group, 4255 West Touhy Avenue, Lincolnwood (Chicago),
Illinois 60646-1975 U.S.A. Originally published by
Hodder and Stoughton Ltd.

Printed and bound in Great Britain by
Butler & Tanner Ltd, Frome and London

CONTENTS

── INTRODUCTION ──

Most of us have, at some time or another, had the urge to cast ourselves adrift in a small boat. For some the dream is of a peaceful day, drifting along on glassy water, while others might choose raging rivers or stormy seas. The canoe makes these dreams possible. Here is an inexpensive travelling craft which can be transported easily to the water of your choice, anywhere in the world. Built to the right specifications it can cruise fast and cleanly, negotiate cataracts and waterfalls or cross oceans.

Unlike most other boats, the canoe is driven by a reliable, efficient and economic engine – the human. It is therefore a quiet-running, pollution-free vessel which causes no disturbance to wildlife and the environment as a whole. Only canoe paddlers can appreciate the harmony this small boat enjoys with the creatures of lake, sea and river. But make no mistake about it, paddling a canoe can be energetic work. Journeying inland, along the coast or through white water, builds upper body strength and whole body endurance. In modern times, when so many people live stressful and pressured lives, these physical benefits, combined with the emotional outlet provided by simple adventuring, are increasingly valued.

Anyone can canoe. The only requirement is that you can find some way to hold a paddle (and for those who can't, the sport may still be enjoyed by travelling in a double). Canoeing is a perfect family sport since the very young through to the very old can get involved, each at their own level. Britain has several thousands of miles of inland waterways and a very accessible coastline, so there is no shortage of water to explore.

The spirit of canoeing is centred on the notion of self-determination – making your own decisions and paddling your own canoe. It's you in control, setting the speed, choosing the route, tackling the difficulties. This represents a special kind of freedom which I think you might find difficult to give up.

The purpose of this book is to guide you towards teaching yourself canoeing. It provides the information you need to get yourself afloat and to be safe while you are out there. The first four chapters should be taken in order because their contents are arranged in a natural learning sequence. The later chapters covering rough water, flat water and sea touring can be tackled however your interest takes you. The final chapter contains the information you will require to carry on learning.

Throughout, key techniques are boxed, to make it easy to refer back to them. Each technique is broken down into logical steps.

I know you will enjoy canoeing and I hope that you will have a great deal of fun learning about it.

The symbols indicate for which type of canoe a particular piece of information is relevant – or whether it is appropriate for both.

 Kayak

 Open canoe

 Kayak and open canoe

1

__BOATS, PADDLES__
AND OTHER BITS

The purpose of this three-part chapter is to help you understand the equipment and boats sufficiently to be able to shop around for the right gear to suit *your own* particular needs. The various pieces of equipment will seem baffling when you first walk into a shop or visit a canoeing event, but with a broad overview of the ways in which the gear is used, you will soon feel confident about choosing your own.

—— What you should know about ——
canoes

◩ *Definitions*

Let's start by getting some important terms sorted out.

Canoeing is a term commonly used to describe the sport, but if we are to be accurate we must recognise the difference between the craft called a *canoe* and the one called a *kayak*. Believe it or not the most universally accepted accurate definition of *canoe* is simply that it is propelled by a single-bladed paddle, which may be used from either a kneeling or a sitting position. A *kayak*, on the other hand, is propelled by a double-bladed paddle used from a sitting position within a space enclosed by a deck known as the *cockpit*.

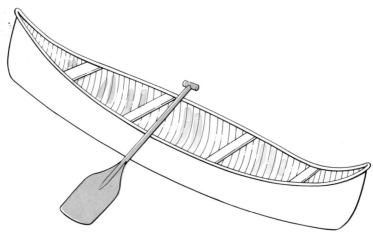

Figure 1.1 The canoe

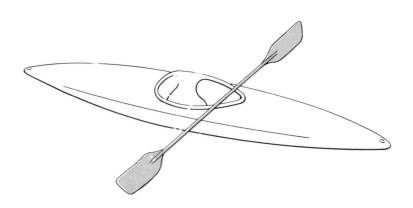

Figure 1.2 The kayak

⊠ Beginnings

The origins of canoeing go back to the first man or woman who straddled a log and drove it through the water using the five-fingered paddles on the ends of his or her arms. The higher tech version of this, of course, had the log's insides hollowed out, its leading end shaped to cut through the water and a sturdy pole for a paddle. *Dugouts* are still used to this day on river and sea by so-called 'primitive' tribes people around the world. The North American Indians took the concept into new dimensions. The massive lakes and extensive river systems which riddled their continent were highways through difficult terrain and the canoe naturally evolved into a portable, lightweight travelling machine. Made from a pinewood frame, covered with sections of bark cut from the abundant birch trees, the canoe could be built and repaired using instantly available materials.

> Thus the Birch Canoe was builded
> In the valley, by the river
> In the bosom of the forest;
> And the forest's life was in it,
> All its mystery and its magic,
> All the lightness of the birch-tree
> All the toughness of the cedar,
> All the larch's supple sinews;
> And it floated on the river
> Like a yellow leaf in Autumn
> Like a yellow water lily.

From *The Song of Hiawatha*, H. W. Longfellow (1855).

In a somewhat different climate, the tough eskimoes could see the advantages of a fast, manoeuvrable and virtually silent boat as a hunting vessel on the sea. Thus the kayak (*hunter's boat* in Inuit) evolved – a deep water craft with a double-bladed paddle which gave the rapid acceleration and deceleration needed for stalking the eskimoes' swimming prey. Seals and walrus were the main quarry and when you consider the size and weight of these huge arctic beasts you can only wonder at the courage and skill of the eskimo in a narrow skin boat.

Man has always been attracted to water for food, for play and for transportation. The popularity of the modern sport of canoeing reflects this fascination. In comparison with larger boats, a canoe or kayak is little more than a small, self-propelled piece of flotsam, but after all these hundreds of years they are still with us. Why? Because they help us to fulfil that tantalising, nagging, wonderful urge to adventure.

Open canoes

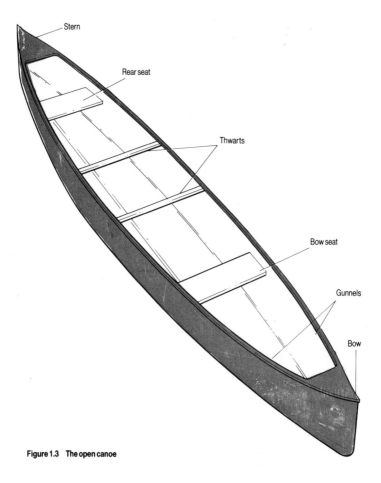

Figure 1.3 The open canoe

The present day descendant of the Indian canoe is referred to as an *open canoe* (implying that it is not covered with a deck like a kayak). The variations in design in modern open canoes are mostly subtle, with the exception of those built especially for racing. The touring boat is usually fitted with two seats and can be paddled quite happily either as a double or as a single. Versatility really is the big attraction of the open canoe. It may be paddled kneeling, sitting or even standing using a pole. It will carry large quantities of equipment or passengers, or a combination of both. A simple sail may be rigged which will carry you downwind or the boat can be filled with flotation to run white water. An open canoe is ideal for the small family wanting one boat to carry everything and everybody. The canoe can be propelled and steered virtually from your first moment on board as a learner. For the beginner who doesn't want to spend too long learning strokes, this makes the open canoe an attractive proposition. That isn't to say that open canoe paddling has no technical components. On the contrary, there is an enormous amount to learn about travelling by canoe. There are also many more sophisticated strokes than are defined in this book.

◢ *Dimensions*

Open canoes are between 4.5 and 6 metres in length and around 90 centimetres in width. Longer boats are obviously more suited to doubles paddling, especially where you intend to carry equipment. A shorter canoe will turn more easily and would be an advantage in descending a rocky river. As always the secret is to try to anticipate what your requirements are likely to be before deciding on a specific boat. Are you more likely to be paddling solo, or do you expect to have another person on board?

Safety features that are essential in an open canoe are:

- Internal flotation
- An end line
- Tangle-free interior

1 Internal flotation
A canoe must be fitted with internal flotation at each end and this must be sufficient to float the whole canoe (filled with water) horizontally at surface level. This means that if for any reason the canoe gets swamped with water it can never sink. The flotation is usually solid foam, either polyethylene or polystyrene. This material must be secured to the interior of the canoe so that it cannot be washed out by water action.

2 An end line
This is a short length of floating line between one and two metres in length attached to one or both ends.

3 Tangle-free interior

The interior of the canoe should be free from any rope, webbing, brackets, etc, which might snag the paddler's legs.

 ## *Construction materials*

Modern canoes are mostly made from plastics of one kind or another, although some are made from aluminium alloy. All of these materials are extremely hardwearing. They will last for many years and survive phenomenal amounts of abrasion and some considerable impacts. The price for this durability is weight. The average weight for a 5 metre canoe constructed in one of the modern plastics is approximately 29 kilograms. Once the canoe has been carried to the water, however, its weight becomes relatively unimportant. In shallow or rocky water, the practically maintenance-free nature of these materials comes into its own. After you've ground over a few gravel banks and scraped along some concrete edges, you'll appreciate the value-for-money argument in favour of plastic boats. Canoes *can* be made lighter but the process and the materials are inevitably more expensive and of course the shell of the boat will not be as tough. Timber and materials such as Kevlar produce magnificently lightweight boats but you will have laid out a lot of money if you purchase one of these beautiful crafts. This will clearly affect your choice of route!

Kayaks

Take a look at any canoeing magazine and you'll see quite clearly that kayaks come in many different shapes and sizes. Basically kayaks are like cars; many will perform general functions adequately, while others are designed with very specialised usage in mind. Let's look at some of the main variables in kayak performance:

- forward speed
- manoeuvrability
- stability
- rough water capability

The first two of these, *speed* and *manoeuvrability*, are the roots of the kayak designer's persistent dilemma. It would be nice to have a kayak which could travel very fast and yet turn on a five pence piece. The truth is of course that such a design is not achievable because the hull-shape requirements for speed and manoeuvrability contradict each other.

Imagine the following models. If you had a pencil floating on water, its long narrow shape and pointed end would let it travel easily and quickly in a straight line forwards. It would not, however, be easy to turn. Now picture a section of watermelon skin floating on the water surface. From this you would get the opposite performance from the pencil. It could spin easily but the curved shape would make it sluggish to push along on a straight course. Try it in the bath – you'll be seeing the two extremes of kayak hull design.

Look at the hull profiles of the kayaks in Figure 1.4 and you can see that boats whose function is straight-line cruising (either racing or touring) have most of their hull length in the water. In other words they have a long keel-line which shows very little upward curve throughout the length. Kayaks designed for manoeuvring (white water, surfing, slalom racing) have short water-lines and curved keels.

Another aspect of speed is width, which is also linked to *stability*. A thin pencil travels more easily through the water than a thick one. But there is a limit to how narrow you can make a kayak. The problem, quite simply, is that narrow kayaks are unstable. You feel that you are sitting balanced on a knife edge and it doesn't take much of an upset to tip you into the water. Fast racing kayaks are narrow and you need to spend a lot of time acquiring the balance to sit and paddle them. Kayaks built with more general activities in mind are much less difficult to balance and some flat water tourers are as stable as a dining-room chair – well almost!

Rough water capability has to take more than hull shape into account. A strong deck and hull are essential because rough water bends and compresses boats with considerable force. Not all rough water kayaks are designed for manoeuvrability; sea touring kayaks and white water racers are concerned with travelling on a mainly straight course. In this case you can guess the hull shape: long water-line length and quite narrow. Decks are contoured to shed breaking waves and are usually high, especially near the bow. This gives greater buoyancy which will cause the boat to rise to the surface through oncoming waves. The total amount of air which a kayak encloses between its deck and hull is referred to as its *volume*.

You can see now that kayak design is mostly about compromise. Any kayak is a collection of performance characteristics. The less extreme the design – in other words the more general its intended usage – the greater will be the degree of compromise in its performance character-istics.

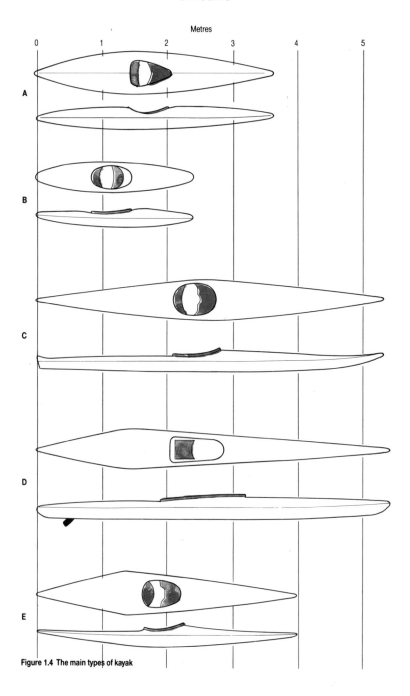

Figure 1.4 The main types of kayak

A White water kayak. Also suitable for surfing, sea trips and flat water touring. Closed cockpit-keyhole type.

B White water play boat used in some extreme situations. Also useful as a pool trainer.

C Sea expedition kayak. Could be used for inland flat water touring.

D Flat water racing K1 (marathon or sprint). Open cockpit. Fast touring flat water kayaks have very similar lines. Rudder may also be on stern.

E Slalom racing K1. Low volume is an important design feature – enabling easier manoeuvering in gates. Being lightweight and fast turning these kayaks can serve as a good introductory boat for youngsters.

Doubles

Two-person kayaks exist, but they are much less common than singles. There are some positive advantages in doubles. For example, the kayak can be kept moving when one paddler is resting or otherwise engaged. This fact, combined with the morale advantages of a 'crew' providing the power, makes the double kayak a serious consideration for long, arduous journeys. Doubles are also useful for helping a less experienced paddler get into locations which might otherwise be out of reach as a single paddler.

Cockpit size

The eskimoes called the cockpit the *manhole*. It's a pretty good description, but not all modern kayak cockpits are a tiny opening in the deck just large enough to let you squeeze in. Kayaks designed for flat water touring and marathon or sprint racing have very large cockpits which leave the paddler's hips and most of his legs out in the open air. This gives maximum freedom of movement and extremely easy access into and out of the kayak. This type of arrangement is usually referred to as an *open cockpit*.

White water kayaks and those used for sea touring have smaller cockpits. There are two main reasons for this. The first is that a smaller 'manhole' is better for keeping water out. The second reason is that a paddler in rough water relies on gripping the inside of the cockpit area with the knees and thighs in order to control the boat's balance. Eskimo rolling after an accidental capsize is only possible if the paddler has this grip on the boat. The paddler is, in fact, literally *wearing* the kayak. These rough water cockpits which enclose the knees are referred to as *closed cockpits*. The term *closed* is not really a fair description, however, as modern white water cockpits are carefully designed to make escape very easy. They are designed on the *keyhole* principle, i.e. the cockpit narrows around the knees but is long enough to let the legs come out easily if they are moved to a central position.

Essential safety features applying to all kayaks

The following checklist shows the safety features which must be present if any kayak is to be safe. There must be absolutely no compromise with these.

- Internal flotation
- Clear cockpit space
- A footrest
- Grab handles

1   Internal flotation

A kayak must be fitted with enough internal flotation to float a fully swamped boat on the surface.

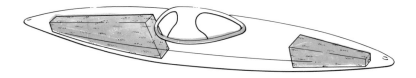

Internal flotation is essential in all kayaks. It usually takes the form of two solid foam blocks. In a polyethylene kayak these would be held in place by brackets screwed onto the kayak's deck.
Other types of flotation exist. Air bags work well on their own or as a way of augmenting buoyancy provided by foam blocks.

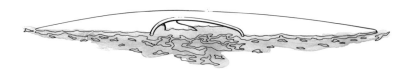

Internal flotation should hold a swamped boat on the surface. Without flotation most kayaks would sink when fully swamped. Foam blocks tend to float the kayak on its side. Additonal flotation (air bags, say) would float this kayak much higher in the water.

Figure 1.5 Internal flotation

2   Clear cockpit space

A cockpit space must be free from rope, string or any other objects which might interfere with the paddler's exit.

3   A footrest

This is essential if you are to be able to paddle efficiently. It also prevents you from sliding forwards if the kayak should make a nose-on impact.

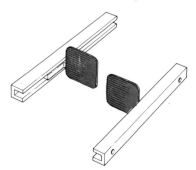

A pedal footrest. The tracks bolt to the boat sides. Each pedal is independently adjustable. The system is safe in easy water

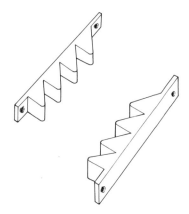

An economy footrest (shark's tooth). Made from plastic mouldings, it provides for a limited number of foot positions. Not suitable for white water.

A typical flat water touring or racing footrest system. The crosspiece of wood, fibre glass or alloy bolts onto two flanges which are moulded in place when the kayak is built. Not suitable for closed cockpit boats.

Figure 1.6 Footrests

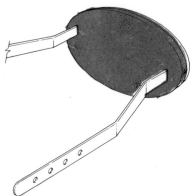

A 'full-plate' footrest which is used for serious white water. Your feet rest on a shock-absorbing foam pad. Adjustment is at the cockpit where the alloy arms fit onto bolts on either side.

4   Grab handles

These are fitted to the ends of your kayak, usually at deck level. They give you something positive to hang onto should you find yourself swimming. Grab handles take different forms – toggles or loops of tape or rope. Providing they are strong these are all OK. If you intend to paddle serious white water, however, you should get more advice on the best type of grab handle to use.

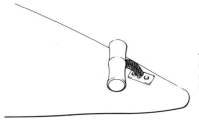

Toggle
May be attached by various means. A toggle is a very safe system provided that the rope or webbing attachment is kept in good condition.

Rope loop
Various forms exist. Some loops can trap a hand or fingers if the kayak spins in rough water or waves.

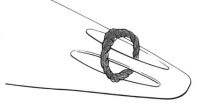

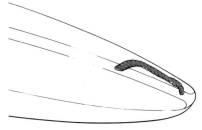

Rope or tape handle
An excellent system. Safe and strong provided the handle is kept in good condition. Good in white water rescue situations where the handle has to be hooked.

Figure 1.7 Types of end grab handles.

◪ *Construction materials*

When we look at the materials from which kayaks are built we see that once again, as with open canoes, there is a trade off between strength, weight and cost. Lightweight racing boats are made from expensive products such as Kevlar. In non-competitive kayaking, weight is much less important and durability, which represents cost-effectiveness, takes on major significance. Kayaks made from moulded polyethylene are the most popular by far. They are immensely resilient and last for years. For this reason they are especially popular with paddlers who want to run white water. For the complete beginner, the robustness of polyethylene combines with its low price to make it a good boat material.

If you intend only to travel on flat water (canal, slow-moving river or lakes) then a fast touring kayak in polyethylene is a reasonable choice. You could, however, get a lighter boat, handbuilt in glass reinforced plastic (glass fibre) without spending a great deal more. Being lighter, it is easier to push along in the water and carrying is much less tiring. You'll have to work at looking after such a boat though, and that includes taking more care of it in transit than would be necessary for a polyethylene version.

One of the things you should always bear in mind is that canoes and kayaks suffer as much, if not more, damage while they are being transported to and from the water as they do actually on the water.

⊠ — Buying your own canoe or kayak —

You will need to buy a boat at some stage but don't be too hasty. My advice is to spend a little time finding out what goes on in canoeing. Where will you be able to get afloat locally? Will you want to get into white water, sea canoeing or competition? Will you be able to transport your boat by car? You should try to talk to some paddlers, read magazines and (modern) books on canoeing so that you get a feel for the different experiences the sport has to offer. There are some good videos available which capture the spirit of the different canoeing disciplines (see chapter 8). Paddlers are friendly people and most will happily let you try out their boats so that you can get some idea of the performance of various designs.

When you decide to buy, go for something which gives you some choice of paddling activity, unless you are absolutely committed to one of the specialist disciplines.

You can save some money by shopping around the retailers before you buy. There aren't that many different types of boat and you can soon compare prices. Watch out for package deals where paddle and spray cover are included – these can be good value. Canoeing magazines like *Canoeist* are packed with advertising and would be a good starting point. In Britain the label of the British Association of Canoe Traders indicates you are probably dealing with a reputable manufacturer or retailer.

Buying used boats

Unlike used cars, which have lots of hidden parts which cannot be inspected, you can nearly always see and get your hands on everything in a used canoe or kayak. This makes secondhand buys quite safe, providing you know what to look for. Here are some tips on what to watch for:

- Any hole or tear in the skin of the boat (deck or hull) which might leak. Repaired holes are likely to be perfectly sound, but check this on the water if you are in doubt.
- Some secondhand boats may have lost their internal flotation foam. You can buy replacement foam and restore the boat but make sure the price you pay allows for this. Never be tempted to use a boat which does not have its full internal flotation.
- Inspect the footrest. Be sure that it can be adjusted to suit your leg length.

Most kayaks can be repaired. Handbuilt fibre glass boats are no problem and boats built in *linear* polyethylene can be heat welded. Some polyethylene boats are built in *cross-linked* plastic which is harder to damage but also harder to repair. A number of manufacturers and retailers offer a repair service. On no account whatsoever should you consider using a kayak on the sea if its hull and deck are not completely watertight. As well as in canoeing magazines, you will find used boats advertised on club noticeboards and at events such as competitions.

—— What you should know about —— paddles

◤ *Kayak paddles*

All paddles have two main parts; the *blades* (two for a kayak, one for a canoe) and the *shaft*. Almost the first thing you will notice about a kayak paddle is that its blades are offset in relation to each other. There are several reasons for this, the main one being that when one blade is pulling in the water the other is trying to slice through the air. It slices much more easily if it is offset. The angle of offset is usually between 90 and 80 degrees although the exact figure is not at all critical until you are doing a lot of paddling. A kayak paddle feels unwieldy and distinctly odd when you first pick one up. Don't worry about this – the shape will soon make sense once you start to use it.

Paddle construction

You could spend a lot of money on a very high specification lightweight racing paddle made from carbon fibre and Kevlar, but in my opinion this is totally unnecessary. Until you have fairly sophisticated paddling skills all that technology will be of little use to you. Start with a simple alloy shafted paddle with moulded plastic blades. These will be light, strong enough, and if looked after should last a couple of years at least. When you do invest in a more expensive pair you'll be glad still to have these as spares.

Two things you should go for when buying a paddle are:

- **Curved blades**. The blades should be moulded into a gentle curve which helps the paddle to grip the water. Don't buy flat blades, you'll very quickly outgrow their performance.
- **Shaped hand-grips**. The paddle shaft should be *ovalled* at the sites where your hands will grip. This is usually plainly visible and you can feel it by rolling the paddle shaft in your grip. The purpose of this ovalling is to help you locate the gripping position without having to look at the blades, which plays an important part in good technique.

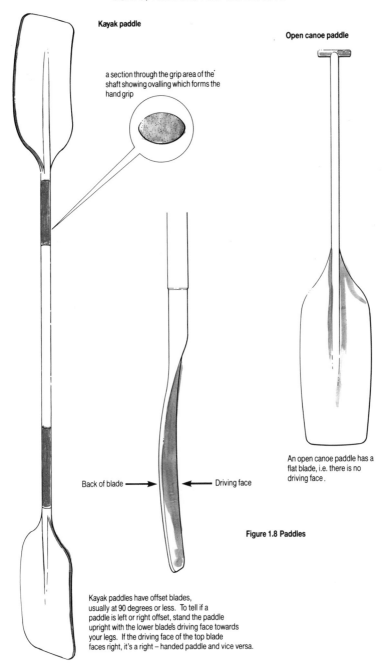

Kayak paddle

Open canoe paddle

a section through the grip area of the shaft showing ovalling which forms the hand grip

Back of blade ➜   ⬅ Driving face

An open canoe paddle has a flat blade, i.e. there is no driving face.

Figure 1.8 Paddles

Kayak paddles have offset blades, usually at 90 degrees or less. To tell if a paddle is left or right offset, stand the paddle upright with the lower blade's driving face towards your legs. If the driving face of the top blade faces right, it's a right – handed paddle and vice versa.

Paddle length

The overall tip-to-tip length of paddles varies between 204 and 220 centimetres. Paddlers who do mostly 'straight-line' paddling such as flat water racers, sea kayakers and inland tourers use longer paddles

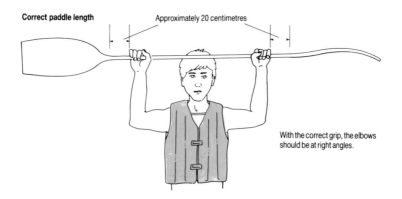

Correct paddle length

Approximately 20 centimetres

With the correct grip, the elbows should be at right angles.

With the canoe paddle, the right angle at the elbows is a good starting grip.

Figure 1.9 Paddle length and grip

while slalom racers, white water kayakers and surfers prefer shorter lengths. Young children, of course, would require paddles of proportionately shorter length. Most manufacturers will supply paddles with shorter shafts if requested.

The precise length of a paddle is not absolutely critical for the beginner, but a simple rule of thumb for a person who wants to do general paddling is to allow 20 centimetres between the heel of your hand and the start of the blade while holding the paddle in the proper grip. A few centimetres either side of this is also fine.

Left- and right-handed grip

Kayak paddles are either left- or right-handed, according to the way the curved blades have been offset against each other. The general rule is that right-handed people prefer right-handed paddles and vice versa. If you are in doubt about your handedness simply stand and paddle in the air with a left and then right paddle and see which feels more comfortable. (See the section on holding the paddle, p. 47).

Caring for your paddle

Try to develop a caring attitude towards your paddle. The quality of the shaft surface in the area of the grips is especially critical, because a small nick or even a roughness can cause an unpleasant sore on your hands. Shafts are particularly vulnerable when you are transporting the kayak and also when you are landing and getting out of the boat. Try to carry your paddles *inside* the car, where they are less likely to be stolen. Never throw your paddles onto a bank from the water and don't use them to sit on as you get into the boat – an old-style method which is still seen in some canoeing literature. Your paddles are your hands – you feel with them and create boat movement with them – so they need to be cared for.

Canoe paddles

Traditionally the open canoe was propelled by a hand-carved wooden paddle, and indeed today the enthusiasts still use beautifully worked timber creations. These paddles have a soft, springy 'feel' in the water and a natural 'life' that is difficult to reproduce in even the most advanced of modern materials. There are at least as many shapes of canoe paddle blade as there are types of open canoe, each with its own special purpose and properties.

Wooden canoe paddles are not at all difficult to get hold of – specialist retailers stock them, but you must remember that wood needs care and maintenance if it is to last. Keeping a wooden paddle is a labour of love and not everybody loves to labour. Canoe paddles built from the same alloy shaft and plastic blade system used in economy kayak paddles are readily available. They are certainly strong enough for the job and would be a good starting paddle for a beginner.

Choosing a paddle

There's less to worry about when buying a canoe paddle. You simply get a blade, shaft and T grip. There are no left- or right-handed problems and all you have to decide on is the length. Stand the paddle vertically in front of you – the T grip should come to about chin height. A few centimetres either way is no serious problem.

Specialist canoeists in white water and those in marathon racing use shorter and longer paddles respectively. In fact, there is little you can't do using one of chin length.

It is possible that you might buy a paddle and find that the T grip comes separately from the shaft. This is quite common and the idea is that you cut the shaft (using a hacksaw) to suit yourself and then glue the grip in place. If you use this system, rough the shaft inside with some emery cloth or coarse glass paper before applying the glue. Use a two-part epoxy adhesive.

—— What you should know about —— other canoeing equipment

Just like almost every other outdoor sport, canoeing has a range of supporting equipment and clothing to adorn the participant. All of this may be fashionable, but I urge you to treat your choice of this equipment just as seriously as you would your choice of boat.

Most canoeing takes place on cold water and often in low air temperatures. Both of these elements are hostile to an unprotected paddler. Most of us are, after all, tropical creatures. With the right clothing and equipment, however, we can play and explore on – and even in – the

water with little discomfort. Once again, you must pay close attention
to your own requirements so that you choose the best gear for your
purpose.

◪ *The buoyancy aid*

A buoyancy aid is a jacket designed to help you stay afloat in the water.
If you are a non-swimmer then you should consider the wearing of
personal buoyancy as absolutely essential (as is learning to swim,
sooner or later). If you can swim quite happily, you should develop the
habit of wearing a buoyancy aid simply as a safeguard against the worst
possible situation where you take a swim in cold water and become
seriously incapacitated by it. As a kayak or open canoe paddler, what
you need is the simplest of canoeing buoyancy aids. Expensive models
with additions such as pockets and chest harnesses are designed with
the leader or extreme expedition paddler in mind. The less expensive
version is just as efficient at keeping you afloat.

A buoyancy aid designed for canoeing will have flotation foam mounted
on both the front and the rear of the jacket. This soft foam is cut in a
way which minimises restriction to your arm movements and has the
added advantage of providing valuable heat insulation to your torso in
cold weather. In some jackets the foam is fitted in narrow, vertical
panels while others use whole 'slabs' in front and rear. Both systems
are effective.

Another design variation is the method of putting the jacket on. Front-
opening by means of a zip and/or buckles is one possibility and pull-
over-the-head is the other. Again, there isn't much in it – the zipped
jacket is easier to get on, but there is always the possibility of the zip
failing. In practice good quality buoyancy aids rarely have zip failure.
Choose the type you feel most comfortable with. There are two main
things to check when you buy a buoyancy aid:

- It should fit well. Try it on with your usual canoeing clothing –
  don't choose one which is oversized as it can be a serious hindrance
  when you swim.
- It should carry the approval of a respected standards agency. In
  Britain this would be any one of the following stamps:
  BCU/BCMA 83
  SBBNF/79
  BMIF Standard

Every buoyancy aid has a securing device of one kind or another which has to be fastened once the jacket has been put on. This is usually at waist level, in the form of a drawcord or buckle. The purpose of this is to help the jacket grip your trunk. (When you are floating in a buoyancy aid you are literally hanging from it.) You should always wear this fully tightened, with the zip (if it has one) fully closed. Securing the jacket when or if you end up in the water sounds like a great idea but it doesn't work. The jacket is difficult to fasten when you are floating and anyway your attention should be on other things.

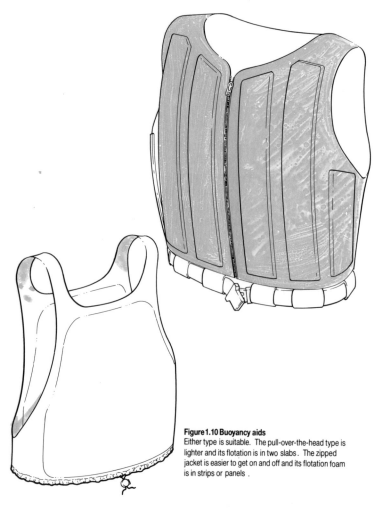

Figure 1.10 Buoyancy aids
Either type is suitable. The pull-over-the-head type is lighter and its flotation is in two slabs. The zipped jacket is easier to get on and off and its flotation foam is in strips or panels .

Clothing

The type of clothing you need for canoeing varies according to the climate and the type of paddling you intend to undertake.

Try to think ahead about the paddling you are going to be doing and analyse what exactly you need from the clothing which you will be wearing. Here are some of the requirements you are likely to come up with:

- Keep me warm by insulating my body heat effectively
- Retain this insulation, or at least most of it, when wet
- Dry quickly at the end of the day or even whilst being worn
- Offer the least possible restriction to my body movements
- Be tough enough to survive the general wear and tear of paddling

You can probably think of others but these are the absolute fundamentals. They can apply to individual garments or to groups of clothing, known as *systems*. Look at the wetsuit – it conforms to all of these requirements but it can perform even more effectively if it is used as part of a clothing system. In other words, combined with a long-sleeved vest and with a canoe cag worn over the top, you have a system which is efficient in wet, dry and windy conditions.

A wetsuit is not the universal answer to canoeing clothing. If it is very unlikely that you will be totally immersed during your paddling then you will find that other insulating clothing is more suitable.

The white water paddler and sea canoeist are both dressing for survival; they must wear clothing which makes it possible to carry on despite many soakings or even a swim. As a beginner you will be working on calm water, close to the shore and, providing the temperature is reasonable you could use some non-specialised clothing as follows:

- A waterproof nylon anorak or cagoule
- A T-shirt and nylon tracksuit top, plus a light woollen sweater for colder days
- A swimming costume, nylon tracksuit trousers (preferably with draw-cord waist (to keep them on if they get soaked)
- Well-fitting training shoes (with short laces)

One of the first things you should buy is a proper canoeing jacket or *canoe cag*. These waterproof nylon jackets are shaped for unrestricted arm movement and have neoprene rubber seals at the wrist, neck and waist. You won't regret buying one of these as it'll get used almost every time you paddle.

Wet suits keep you warm if you are immersed in water or soaked by breaking waves. In sea touring and white water paddling they provide essential protection from cold.
A wet suit is hard-wearing and good value for money.

Wet suit boots are not essential unless you are doing a lot of wading in cold water.
For the white water paddler or surfer they really are worth having.

A canoe cag is an essential piece of outer clothing for any canoeist, being windproof *and* waterproof. You will probably get wet under a cag in very rough water but it will still keep you warm.

Figure 1.11 Clothing for canoeing

A thermal vest will be useful in any weather. In colder weather a fibre pile or fleece sweater on top works well – especially if you expect to get soaked.

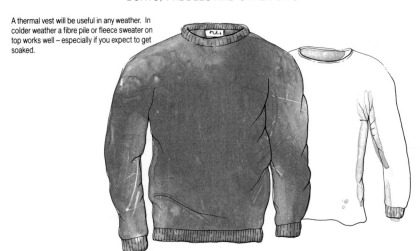

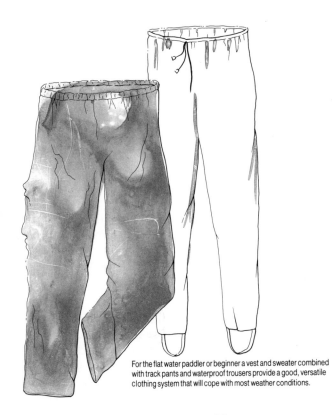

For the flat water paddler or beginner a vest and sweater combined with track pants and waterproof trousers provide a good, versatile clothing system that will cope with most weather conditions.

Wetsuits

If you are intending to get into any kind of rough water canoeing, a wetsuit will be an important investment. Immersion in cold water, or even just soakings from spray, will cool you quickly, but with a wetsuit covering your legs and trunk you can work quite happily for a long time.

Wetsuits are made from a synthetic foam rubber called neoprene which is very buoyant. The suit is skin tight and yet very flexible and only a thin layer of water comes between your skin and the neoprene. The foam has high heat-insulating properties, so you remain wet but warm. A canoeing wetsuit will normally have neoprene of 3 millimetres thickness and will be one piece, i.e. full-length trousers and sleeveless top. In cold weather, paddlers usually wear a vest or sweater under their wetsuit.

Wetsuits are very hardwearing and cuts or tears can be easily repaired using a neoprene adhesive.

Warm clothing and windproofing

I have listed the basic clothing you would need in order to get started in canoeing. Here are some useful tips for improving your clothing once you become more involved in the sport.

The following are some examples of garments which perform well on their own or as a part of a clothing system.

Polypropylene undergarments

These come in vests and long-johns. They are extremely light, dry very quickly indeed and have outstanding 'stretchability'. Virtually every canoeist ends up with a long-sleeved polypropylene vest, their durability and performance making them really good value for money.

Fibre pile clothing

This is a polyester fabric with a furry feel on the inside. It is excellent as an insulation in the form of pullovers and trousers. For cold weather paddling it's hard to beat, because it is very durable and quick to dry. If you do get soaked it remains warm and comfortable. Pile garments are not windproof, however, so you must equip yourself with an outer layer which is. Your canoe cag is perfect for the top half and a pair of waterproof overtrousers will do for the bottom. Fibre pile clothing is readily available in outdoor shops.

Fleece clothing is a more expensive alternative to fibre pile. It is slightly less bulky and more fashionable, but performs superbly as an insulator.

An alternative cold-weather paddling system to the wetsuit would thus be, starting with the inside:

- Polypropylene vest
- Fibre pile top and bottoms
- Canoe cag and overtrousers
- Footwear

⊠ Footwear

It's not unknown to get your feet wet while canoeing! Wading into the water is sometimes a necessary part of getting afloat or landing. In warm weather a pair of training shoes is perfectly adequate so long as they are well secured, but do keep the laces short in case they tangle on something inside the canoe or kayak. Bare feet really are not the answer because of the danger of treading on something which would cause a nasty cut. In cold weather, wetsuit bootees are superb. You can wade in cold water all day and not even notice it. Plenty of people have managed, however, with a pair of short woollen socks inside training shoes.

⊠ Paddle mitts

Canoeing is pretty energetic exercise and you generate heat even with steady gentle paddling. However, you can get days in winter when a cold headwind numbs your fingers. The answer to this is *paddle mitts*, a piece of equipment so simple you'll hardly believe they work.

The mitts are made of basic waterproofed, lightweight nylon. The mitts are attached to the paddle by folding them around the shaft and back onto velcro fastening. The two mitts hang semi-permanently on the shaft. It is easy to get your hands in and out of the mitts as they do not seal tightly around your wrists. Inside they create a welcoming micro-climate on a cold day. Paddle mitts work in white water or flat. They are inexpensive to buy or, if you have a sewing machine and some scrap nylon material, very easy to make.

Making paddle mits

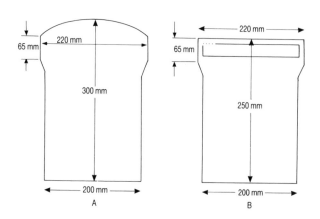

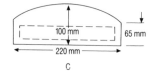

Figure 1.12 Making paddle mits

- Use any proofed nylon (old spray deck or overtrousers?).
- For one mitt cut three pieces to the dimensions shown.
- Sew 1″ velcro to proofed side of C and outer of B.
- Lay the curves of A and C on top of each other, pin and sew the curves together.
- Lay B in position on top of A (both with proofed side outermost). Pin and sew the two side seams as far as the 65mm openings.
- Turn the whole lot the right way out and voilà – one warm hand!

Kayak spray deck

A spray deck is a flexible waterproof skirt which you put on with the other paddling clothing. Once you are in the kayak, the outer edge of the elasticated skirt is snapped over the cockpit rim so that water washing over the decks cannot enter the kayak. A spray deck is essential if you are going to encounter any rough water, as you would while sea touring or running white water. On cold winter days a spray deck is great to have even on flat water, keeping the relatively inactive lower half of your body warm and snug. For this reason you really should get one, regardless of the type of kayak you choose.

The simplest and cheapest spray decks are made from nylon of about 8 ounce quality, backed with waterproofing. I suggest you go for a neoprene-proofed material – the durability far outweighs the slight increase in cost. These spray decks are adequate for all but serious white water. Here are some things to look for when buying a spray deck:

- Fit
- Release strap
- Good waist-tube fit
- Sealed seams

Fit

You must check that the spray deck fits your particular kayak. Try it out. It should grip the cockpit rim firmly and the waist tube should be centred over the seat. Remember, all kayak cockpits are not the same size.

Release strap

The spray deck must have a loop or handle which is used to pull the elasticated skirt edge off the cockpit rim.

Good waist-tube fit

The tube which you step into must be pulled up to about nipple height. Make sure it fits or is adjustable to your size.

Sealed seams

All the seams should be sealed.

Spray decks made from neoprene are for use in white water and on the sea. They give a much superior seal both around the cockpit and around your chest. This type would be a worthwhile investment only if you are committed to paddling white water or sea.

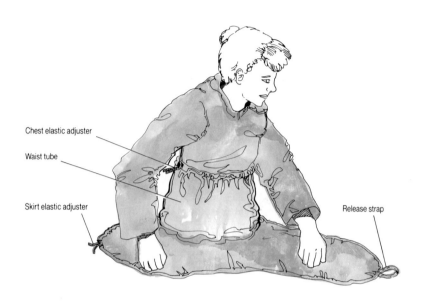

Chest elastic adjuster

Waist tube

Skirt elastic adjuster

Release strap

A spray deck keeps the heat in and the water out. This spray deck has an adjustable chest elastic and skirt elastic. If you can get one which fits you and your kayak these adjusters are unnecessary. Open cockpit spray decks are bigger and have more baggy skirts to allow your knees to be raised.

Figure 1.13 Kayak spray deck

Helmet

If you are contemplating paddling in white water or surf you should wear a canoeing helmet. Paddlers rarely hit their heads, even in the worst of rapid rivers, but as long as the possibility exists it would be very unwise indeed to take the risk of a head injury. A paddling helmet should:

- Fit your head snugly
- Be secured by a strong chin strap
- Have a hard outer shell which covers your forehead and temples

In flat water touring, using either a kayak or open canoe, there is no need for this kind of protection – a woollen ski hat in winter and sun hat in summer would be much more appropriate.

⊠ *Glasses*

If you normally wear glasses then it is best to keep them on while canoeing. Being able to see is quite important – essential in white water. Obviously plastic lenses are safest and being lighter are more comfortable. Paddlers who wear glasses normally secure them with a small elastic strap which pushes onto the ends of the ear pieces, forming a band across the back of the head. These are usually made from neoprene and are inexpensive. Most sports shops sell them.

⊠ *Sun cream*

On sunny days you will need to protect your skin with a suitable sun cream. Make sure that you remove all traces of it from your hands before getting hold of the paddle.

2

PREPARING FOR THE WATER

The purpose of this chapter is to provide you with some practical tips on things you really have to get organised *before* getting to grips with actually paddling your canoe on the water. The intention is to help you get yourself paddling as quickly and as safely as possible. These tips will encourage you to develop good habits from the start in transporting the canoe, personalising it and getting in and out. It will also show you how to handle the paddle, so that you can start thinking about this even before getting afloat. The correct seating position is covered as are the efficient methods of emptying a boat when it takes water on board. Apart from building a sound platform for beginning your learning, this section also contains important safety quidelines. Read it carefully.

—— Carrying and lifting boats ——

You don't have to look far to find canoeists with bad backs, as there are plenty of us around. Paddling an open canoe or a kayak is extremely good exercise for the musculature and joints of the whole trunk, including the lower back. It builds strength and promotes flexibility, two vital ingredients for a healthy back, so why the jolly band of groaning paddlers?

Quite simply they (I should say 'we') have not given proper attention to the way boats are lifted and carried. The human back is immensely strong but the geometry of its construction is such that improper lifting and walking posture can cause it to be overloaded with even the smallest of weights.

Canoeing is fun and moving boats around probably isn't – very often the prospect of getting into the water overrules our instinct to take it steadily. But boats are usually heavy, awkward loads which need to be handled correctly if they are to be moved safely. To make matters worse they often have water on board which is not only heavy but also a very unstable load. I urge you to take serious heed of the advice for picking up and carrying boats which follows.

◪ *Two-up method*

The two-up method of carrying is the safest for a kayak but care is needed to ensure that the slippery surface of the boat doesn't slide from your grip like a block of soap. If you choose to carry by the end-grabs or toggles, check first that they are strong. Both your partner and, closer to home, your big toe can get a nasty shock if a handle snaps while you are carrying a heavy kayak.

Move slowly and steadily when carrying your boat since the rear person has a restricted view of the ground immediately ahead.

Two-up is the wise way to move an open canoe. These boats are a particularly difficult shape to manage alone being both long *and* wide. One person on either side of the boat (holding the gunnels or thwarts) is the way to organise the carry. This lets the boat travel in a balanced position and has the advantage of giving the rearmost person a clear view of the ground ahead.

▨ *Suitcase carry*

This is a comfortable method for carrying a kayak provided it isn't extremely heavy. First prop the kayak up on its edge with the hull leaning against your outside calf. Grip the cockpit at the point of balance with bent knees (usually just forward of the seat side-support) and stand up. Let the carrying arm hang straight and keep an eye on the rear of the boat if you turn around corners or where there are other people around.

Two-up carry
Safe and good when the kayak is heavy.

Suitcase carry
Comfortable once you have found the point of balance.
Good for light boats.

Paddles
inside

Figure 2.1 Carrying canoes and kayaks

Shoulder carry
Best for long solo carries. It gets the kayak away from
your legs, so you can deal with all terrain.

Paddle for
walking stick

Open canoes tend to be heavy. Wherever possible two
people should carry them. If you have no one to help, it
may be possible to use the solo carry. 1. Stand the canoe
on one end. 2. Work your way backwards. 3. Rest the
thwart across your shoulders, rock your weight forwards
and walk.

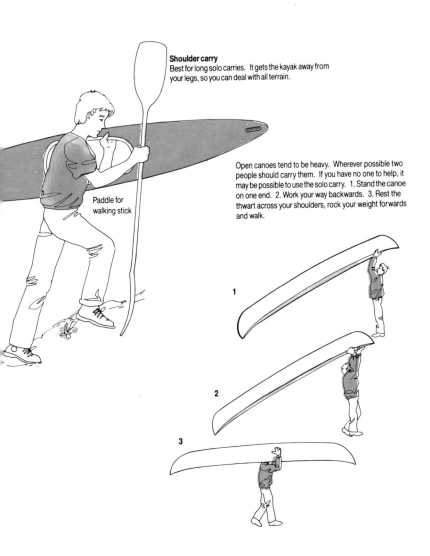

✖ *Shoulder carry*

This is the method most paddlers will use if they have to walk more than 10 or 20 metres. The load is taken on the shoulder, leaving the legs unhindered and one hand free to carry the paddle.

Set the kayak on its edge. Get your feet tucked well in under the boat and then lift it onto the upper part of your thighs. With the weight of the kayak held mainly on your thighs, your next move is to get a shoulder into the cockpit. This is done by catching the cockpit edge furthest away from you with one hand and rolling the kayak upwards and onto the shoulder on that side. Once you have it up there shuffle the cockpit forwards or rearwards until the boat is balanced comfortably. Your technique will improve with this method and soon you'll be able to do it in one smooth movement. Sore shoulder? That'll improve too once you've done a few carries. Use this method to carry your kayaks around canal locks and watch the look of envy on the face of narrow boat skippers!

The shoulder carry for an open canoe is somewhat different, and you will need strong shoulders and a sense of humour. The idea is to balance the centre thwart across the rear of your neck and shoulders. Your head is inside the canoe and your hands are on the gunnels. Vision (albeit restricted) is achieved by tilting the boat upwards at the front. Don't try to use this method in a crowded street where decapitation of fellow pedestrians is a distinct possibility.

A strong person working with a light canoe can roll the boat into position from a sideways lift, similar to the kayak shoulder carry. A much less risky method is to stand at one end of the canoe and then lift and roll it to a hull-uppermost position, leaving the other end resting on the ground. You then back into the canoe, working your way towards the centre thwart which is hitched across your shoulders. Seesaw the boat down at the front until the rear is off the ground and away you go. The committed solo paddlers have a simple method of lashing two paddles across two thwarts which makes the load-bearing on the shoulders much more comfortable in this method of carrying.

Here is a simple checklist of general tips relating to lifting and carrying boats to help you stay healthy:

- Get as much water out as possible before attempting to lift the whole boat – sponge it dry and *then* start to carry.
- Always begin a lift with feet as close as you can get them to the boat – under it if possible.
- Lift using the strength of your thighs and keep a straight back.
- Roll the boat onto its edge to start with.
- Check end-grabs before using them to lift the boat.
- Remember to bend your knees when lifting.
- Watch out when you are on land and the boat is on the water – be prepared to lift the boat by one end and drag the rest onto the shore.

Use this method only with light boats until you are confident in your strength and technique. Remember: You can't paddle with a sore back.

Sponge the boat dry and then roll it onto its edge. Get your feet close underneath it.

Using your thighs, lift the kayak until it rests on your thigh. Hook a hand under the far cockpit rim.

Roll and lift the kayak so that the cockpit rim drops onto your shoulder. Bend at knees to pick up paddle or learn to hook it into your hand with a foot!

Figure 2.2 Picking up a kayak

Launching

If a kayak is heavy, get it on or off the water by sliding it across the bank, end first. Remember to keep hold while launching! This system is used for open canoes too.

Always crouch by bending your legs when picking up (or launching) a kayak. Use the strong muscles of your thighs to do the lifting and lowering, not your back.

Figure 2.3 Launching

Transporting by car

Get used to carrying your canoe or kayak by car. Taking it with you to interesting places and leaping into it when the mood takes you is part of the thrill. Some keen paddlers never take their boats off the roof, except to go on the water or to get into multi-storey car parks.

⊠ *Roof racks*

My advice is to get a good quality roof rack. It won't mark your car's paintwork and most are easy and quick to remove when they aren't needed. A two-part roof rack consisting of two separate cross bars is the best system and you should fix these as far apart as your roof will permit. Choose a strong roof rack – those whose supporting legs are made from cast alloy are extremely good. In the days when all cars had rain gutters on the roof edges a roof rack was a simple and almost universal piece of kit. Unfortunately modern cars rarely have gutters and roof rack clamping devices have become more specialised. However, good strong racks are available for most cars and they remain effective for many years. If you feel the urge to economise on a roof rack, have a long hard think about the forces involved when you brake, go around bends and pass oncoming lorries on windy days.

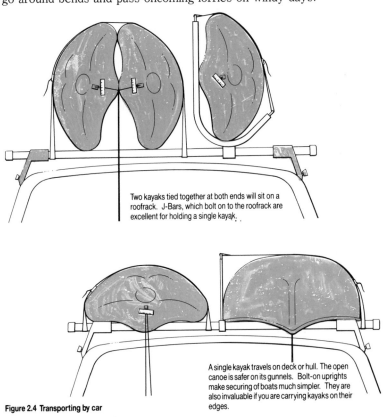

Two kayaks tied together at both ends will sit on a roofrack. J-Bars, which bolt on to the roofrack are excellent for holding a single kayak.

A single kayak travels on deck or hull. The open canoe is safer on its gunnels. Bolt-on uprights make securing of boats much simpler. They are also invaluable if you are carrying kayaks on their edges.

Figure 2.4 Transporting by car

Here are some hints for securing boats on roof racks:

- Open canoes travel best on their gunnels, i.e. hull uppermost. Kayaks are happy either way up unless the decks are flimsy.
- Bolt-on uprights, J-bars and V-bars which attach to the standard racks are kinder to boats and prevent lateral movement of the boat on your roof.
- Use strong, synthetic rope to hold boats on or get some self-locking straps. If you use a rope, learn and use simple reliable knots like the *round turn and two half hitches*.
- Tie off the end-grabs of the boat to strong anchor points on the car front and rear (towing loops are the best points). Tests show that badly-secured roof racks can tear off in even low-speed impacts, turning your canoe into a deadly missile.
- Watch out for kayaks filling with rain water on the roof. Upside down transportation avoids this or you can use your spray deck on the cockpit and close it with a rubber band around the waist tube.*
- Check the load regularly on long runs. The tension on securing ropes and straps is often lost as the boats settle onto the roof rack supports.
- Remember about your extra height. Multi-storey car parks are probably out. It's worth measuring the overall height and keeping a note in metric and imperial units somewhere near your dashboard.

  Also be aware of overhang at front and rear. A white rag tied to the boat end at the rear helps you judge distance while reversing.

▨ *Trolleys*

Several firms make trolleys for canoes and kayaks. For the solo paddler with a heavy boat these can be an important consideration. The trolley is normally two-wheeled and mounted on alloy tubing, carrying a simple securing strap. It is best to choose a trolley that folds into a size which allows it to be carried in the boat. On very rough ground a trolley is of limited use and a heavy boat may have to be sledged over the ground. On grass or heather this is no problem, but over anything rougher, such as sand or gravel, the abrasion can cause considerable wear. Under these conditions, if carrying is out of the question, you'll be glad you saved those strips of carpet that are stashed away in the loft.

Getting the paddling position right

Before you get afloat spend some time sitting in your canoe or kayak on dry land. Pick an area of flat grass to rest your boat on.

◢ *Open canoe*

First try out the seated position. Remember, when you are going solo you use the bow seat but face the rear of the boat for this. (This places you closer to the canoe's centre – better for solo control.) Sitting on the seat with your feet on the floor might feel okay but a more business-like position for paddling is to tuck one foot underneath the seat and rest the knee on the floor. The other leg is stretched out straight in front. This is a remarkably comfortable position for long, gentle touring and you can alternate from one stretched-out leg to the other as much as you like.

For a little more stability you can go onto both knees, keeping part of your bottom resting on the seat. Try swapping between these positions in the boat on dry land so that you are familiar with them when you get afloat.

Now try the mid-solo position, the one you will use to learn the steering strokes. You should be to one side of the boat with the centre thwart just in front of you. If you feel that your knees are going to get sore, or if the floor is very slippery, now is the time to glue some foam padding onto where your knees will rest. Choose tough foam like polyethylene, the kind sold in camping shops as sleeping mats. Around 10 millimetres is the right thickness. Cut this to the size required and then rough the surface of the plastic with coarse glasspaper. Glue the foam with waterproof impact adhesive.

◢ *Kayak*

One thing you must do first in this dry land preparation is to adjust your footrest. Having your feet positioned correctly plays an important part in your overall efficiency. Don't be tempted to paddle without a footrest: it places unnecessary strain on the groin muscles and in white water or surf is extremely dangerous if you hit something head-on.

A very popular and comfortable position for flat touring. The seat is used to support part of your weight. Alternate the bent knee as you please.

Kneeling on both knees is more stable – for rougher water maybe.

The mid-solo position is the most stable and gives greater control when turning. The canoe sits slightly tipped to one side.

Figure 2.5 Paddling positions in the open canoe

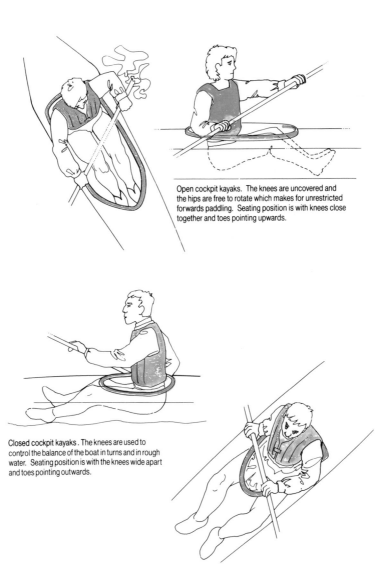

Open cockpit kayaks. The knees are uncovered and the hips are free to rotate which makes for unrestricted forwards paddling. Seating position is with knees close together and toes pointing upwards.

Closed cockpit kayaks. The knees are used to control the balance of the boat in turns and in rough water. Seating position is with the knees wide apart and toes pointing outwards.

Figure 2.6 Kayak seating positions

Footrests come in different shapes and forms (see Figure 1.6, p. 12). If you are a beginner, any type will do as long as it can be adjusted to suit your leg length and is firm and comfortable. Always set a footrest so that your legs are bent at the knees. This helps to give you some 'push' against the footrest while paddling. You might not realise it at first, but a kayak is driven along by your feet. As each paddle blade grips the water the foot on that side thrusts the boat forwards. The angle at which your knees should be flexed is not at all critical, you should simply find what feels most comfortable. Once you've settled on a footrest setting which feels good on dry land you can make finer alterations later, when you've done some paddling.

Sitting in the 'open' cockpit

Flat water touring kayaks as well as those designed for marathon racing have long, wide cockpits. The sitting position is with knees raised and together. Only your bottom, heels and the soles of your feet are in contact with the kayak – thus giving you a great deal of freedom to move as you paddle. This is a big help if you plan to cover miles on placid rivers or lakes.

Sitting in the 'closed' cockpit

A 'closed' cockpit allows you to grip the kayak with your knees. Your legs should lie apart with knees flexed and in contact with the underside of the deck. Notice that this is exactly opposite to the knees together position used with the open cockpit. Adjust the footrest until you can sit in this position with your legs relaxed. Once you've done some paddling it might well be necessary to make further fine adjustments before you are completely happy.

Tailoring the seat and cockpit

If you plan to use your kayak to learn white water techniques you will need to think about another point of contact with the cockpit – the hips. When you sit in the boat at first there will probably be a space between your hips and the seat-sides. This space should be padded out using strips of foam glued onto the seat side-supports. Polyethylene camping mat type foam is best. Polyethylene foam turns up in all sorts of places. Don't confuse it however with polystyrene foam which is much more common. Polyethylene foam is more expensive, remains intact when you bend and twist it and doesn't squeak when you rub it. It's about 10 millimetres thick and will glue well with waterproof, impact adhesive applied to both surfaces. (Rough the plastic surface up well with coarse glass paper before applying the adhesive.) Build up layers until you get a comfortable fit. Remember to tailor the padding to fit you with your usual paddling clothes on – wearing a wetsuit will make you a good deal wider in the hips than track pants will. If you have thin legs which don't easily reach the knee-grip area,

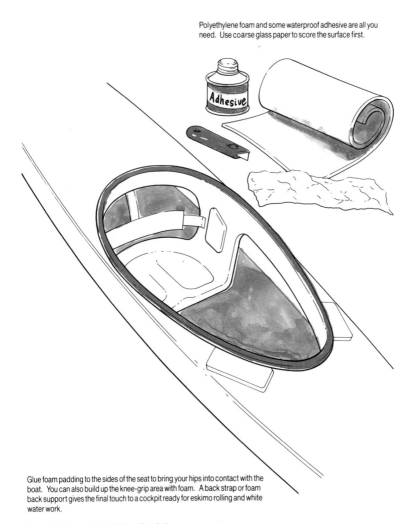

Polyethylene foam and some waterproof adhesive are all you need. Use coarse glass paper to score the surface first.

Glue foam padding to the sides of the seat to bring your hips into contact with the boat. You can also build up the knee-grip area with foam. A back strap or foam back support gives the final touch to a cockpit ready for eskimo rolling and white water work.

Figure 2.7 Personalising the closed cockpit

you can use the same foam to build up the underside of the deck/ cockpit. Here you will be building downwards with the foam padding, towards the floor of the kayak.

Don't be apprehensive about making these alterations to your new boat; it really is worth doing. You will be much more comfortable as a result and the kayak will begin to feel a part of you. In white water, that's exactly the kind of feeling you want so that your hip and knee movements are transmitted immediately into the boat. Don't worry about doing irreparable damage to the seat interior; the adhesive and foam padding will not harm the plastic and can very easily be ripped out if you make a mistake. If the padding is a little oversized in places it is easy to thin and trim using a very sharp knife. A carving knife is quite good for this, allowing you to shave pieces off here and there.

———————— Handling the paddle ————————

◢ *The open canoe paddle*

The open canoe paddle is extremely simple to use. Just pick it up by the shaft and place one hand over the T-grip. Now work out the spacing between your hands by putting the shaft on top of your head and moving the other hand until you get a right angle formed at both elbows. (See also chapter 1, figure 1.9, p. 18)

This is simply a guide to get you started. You'll soon find that the lower hand takes up other positions on the shaft for various strokes. In sweep strokes for example, you might find that the lower hand moves slightly towards the T-grip. Practise the J stroke (see chapter 3, p. 96) in the air before you get afloat so that your arms and wrists get accustomed to the basic action *before* you get into the canoe.

In water which becomes too shallow to give a decent purchase with the blade, the open canoe paddle can be used to *pole* off the bottom. This is very effective but as you might imagine, soon takes its toll if you are using an expensive wooden paddle. When you really get into open canoe work you can learn the proper poling technique. This is done standing up in the canoe and using a pole about 4 metres in length to drive off the river bed. It's a method that can be used either to ascend or descend shallow rapids and is just another indication of the tremendous versatility of the open canoe as a journeying vehicle.

The kayak paddle

To establish the width of your grasp on the paddle shaft, place the mid-point of the shaft on top of your head and move your hands to a position which gives a right angle at each elbow. Once you have done this, hold the paddle out in front of you at arm's length to check that your hands are spaced equally from the centre. It's a good idea to mark the inner limit of each hand's grip with some coloured PVC tape. This allows you to check at a glance while you are paddling that your hold on the shaft is evenly spaced. (See also chapter 1, pp. 18–19.) Beginners are often seen paddling, unknowingly, with a large piece of shaft showing on one side and virtually none on the other.

Feathering

The action of turning the paddle blades with each stroke so that they enter the water *square* to the direction of pull is called *feathering* and the angle at which the blades are offset to each other is usually referred to as *the feather*. When you are a complete beginner, feathering is a nuisance and it's hard to see any real point to it. Well, as is often the case when you are learning, it's worth persevering. Feathered paddles make it possible for you to move faster and they are actually ergonomically better for the kayaking action than non-feathered paddles.

A good way to get started with feathering is to do some paddling in the air. Sitting on a stool or standing up is fine for this. Imagine that the water level is around the level of your bottom and then take up your paddles in the proper grip. The following instructions are for a right-handed person with right-handed paddles.

Feathering

- Drop the right blade into the (imaginary) water and pull to your hip.
- Lift the right blade out.
- When the right blade comes out use your right hand to swivel the shaft so that the left blade is set to grip the water. The left hand goes slack, allowing the shaft to swivel. The right hand swivel is done by bringing the knuckles upwards (like accelerating on a motorcycle).
- Pull with the left blade to the hip.
- Lift out the left blade.
- Swivel the shaft again so that the right blade is ready to enter the water. (Again grip and swivel with the right hand – let it slip in the left.)

Left-handers using left-handed paddles simply do the gripping with the left hand and let the shaft swivel in the right. It isn't complicated; a paddler moving quickly is doing it several times per second.

You will learn feathering very quickly and after your first day on the water you'll probably forget that it's happening. Your forearms may ache a little in the first few days but again you will adapt to it in a remarkably short time. You will probably notice a distinct strengthening of these gripping muscles of your forearm in the first few months of paddling.

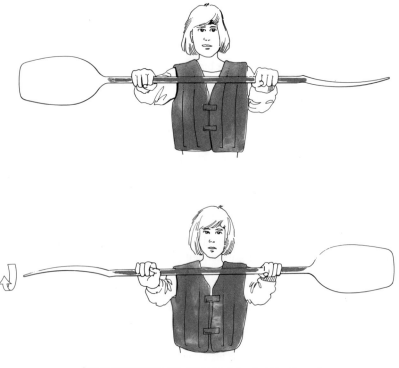

Feathering a right control paddle. The right hand grips – the left hand loosens its grip to allow the shaft to swivel.

Figure 2.8 Feathering the kayak paddle

— Getting into and out of the boat —

Getting into canoes has provided material for slapstick film makers for years, the best one being the left foot sailing off into the sunset while the right foot remains very much a landlubber. Entertaining people, however, is likely to be the last thing in your head when you make your first attempt to get aboard. Care is certainly needed, but if you follow the guidance given below it will soon give you no more trouble than getting on a bike.

The first important message about getting in is to make life easy by picking the right spot. Ideally you want a straight piece of bank about 15 centimetres above the water surface (a lot higher or a lot lower does make it harder). The idea is to put the smallest possible distance between the edge of the bank and the place where you intend to sit in the canoe or kayak.

Open canoes

Canoes are very easy to get into once you've found a good spot.

Getting into an open canoe

- Lay your paddle alongside the boat.

- Crouch down on your heels, close to the edge, with your hands on the ground.

- Reach out with the nearest leg and place your foot into the middle of the boat, keeping your weight over the bank (on your other leg and arm).

- Place a hand on the centre of the thwart and, without standing up straight, drop quickly into the bottom of the boat with the other leg.

Getting out is a reversal of this. The secret is to keep low while you transfer your weight from canoe to bank. Set your paddle onto the bank first just in case the canoe drifts off and you need an improvised boat hook!

Kayaks

One of the simplest ways to get into a kayak is to start from a beach which shelves gradually into the water. Set the kayak down on the area which is just awash with water and simply get in. The boat will be resting on the bottom, so now you shuffle your way forward with a hand on the ground on either side (like a seal in fact!). One method which is used from a bank (rather than a beach) and is much kinder to the hull of your kayak is as follows:

Getting into a kayak

- With the boat floating alongside a straight piece of bank, lay the paddle down so that it will be within reach once you are on board.

- Crouch low on your heels, one arm on the bank and the other on the front of the cockpit.

- Keeping your weight on the bank foot and arm, step into the cockpit with the near foot.

- Keeping one hand on the bank, swing your other foot into the boat and sit down quickly. Keep your weight low throughout.

Getting out of a kayak

- Pull up close to the bank and set the paddle on shore.

- Pull your knees up until your heels are as close as possible to your seat.

- Place one hand on the front of the cockpit and the other on the bank and pull yourself onto your feet.

- Keeping your weight low, step out quickly.

If you are working with a closed cockpit kayak you might find that you need to add one more stage to the above systems. This simply involves sitting on the back of the cockpit rim while transferring your weight between the bank and the kayak. While getting in, sit on the rim first and then shuffle both legs into the boat. (You will probably prefer to transfer the hand from the front of the cockpit to a point directly behind your bottom.) Finally, bump off the rim onto the seat. Reverse the process to get out.

——————— Emptying ———————

You'll have to empty your boat many times in the future. It's a good habit to drain it completely before you get afloat each time so that it is as light and responsive as possible. There are two main ways of emptying. One is where you want to get rid of a small quantity of water (a few litres or less) which has come in through splashing or off your feet. The second is where the boat has taken a massive amount of water on board, as in the case of a capsize.

The simplest way to get rid of small quantities of water is to use a sponge. It might sound ridiculous but this is a good method, capable of shifting a few litres of water in a very short time *and* it allows you to get every last drop out. Tip the kayak or canoe onto one edge when you are sponging; this makes the water form a deep pool which can be quickly sucked up by the sponge. An ordinary synthetic bath sponge is ideal for the job – it's inexpensive, it floats and it can be stored by compressing it into some out-of-the way space in the boat such as under the seat.

A sponge can save you a lot of hard work but to get rid of large quantities of water, you're faced with actually picking the boat up and swilling it out, as described below.

Open canoes

If possible get help first. If the boat is lying swamped in the water turn it onto its edge and slowly raise the ends. The water will flow out quite happily as long as you create the slightest gradient with the canoe. You may reach a point where there is still some water onboard which refuses to flow over the gunnel and out of the boat. Once you have as much out as possible take the canoe ashore and move the rest of the water by sponge. If you have to work alone get the canoe onto its side and raise it slowly by gripping the centre thwart and using your shoulder underneath the gunnel. See figure 2.9 on page 52.

Kayaks

If you have taken the trouble to fit your kayak with air bags in addition to the standard, fitted flotation, the boat will be very much easier to handle when it becomes swamped. The reason for this will be obvious; the air bags and foam flotation take up so much space inside the kayak that only the cockpit area is free to fill with water. In the sea or white water, excluding water in this way takes on a serious, life-preserving importance. The procedure for emptying a heavily swamped kayak is as follows:

Emptying a swamped kayak

- Get the kayak into shallow water but leave it in the water.

- Roll it onto its side. In very shallow water this in itself will dislodge a lot of water.

- Stand in the water – one person holding each end.

- Raise the ends until you start a flow out of the cockpit.

- Simply maintain this steady flow by slowly raising the ends one at a time until no more water will come out.

- Turn the boat over completely, clear of the water, and raise one end slightly so that water spills out. Repeat a few more times and then lift it ashore and finish the job with a sponge.

Work carefully when dealing with a fully swamped boat. Do only the minimum of lifting necessary. You don't have to lift water high into the air above your head in order to get it out of the kayak, a lift of a few centimetres is enough to start the flow.

If you are working alone with an open canoe get one shoulder under the gunnel and/or use the centre thwart to help you lift.

Figure 2.9 Emptying an open canoe

If you are working alone with a swamped boat, start the flow from the cockpit by standing astride it and raising it slowly. When the flow ends flip the kayak over onto its hull where it will now float reasonably high. Go to one end and push the boat until a low bank will support one end. Turn it upside down and raise and lower the other end to get the remainder out. Sponge the last dribble out as usual.

Another way to get rid of the last bit that won't come out with the edge-ways lift is to get the kayak right way up and depress one end so that water rushes down to it. Next, quickly raise that end out of the water and at the same time turn the boat upside down. Water will pour from the cockpit and you can repeat the whole action as often as is necessary. This system works well in the swimming pool and situations where you may be emptying in waist-deep water.

Open cockpit kayaks will drain very easily once on their edge, and really present no problems provided you stick to the advice about getting a flow and not lifting water and boat unnecessarily high.

Don't remove a swamped boat from the water. Roll it onto its edge in shallow water – if a flow out of the cockpit doesn't start, raise the ends gradually. A few inches is all that is needed.

To get the last 'slops' out place one end on a low bank and raise the other end enough to run water out of the cockpit.

Figure 2.10 Emptying a swamped boat

Sponging is a sensible way to get the boat dry – you only lift the water not the boat.

Figure 2.11 Sponging

Emptying in deep water

This is virtually impossible to do alone, with the exception of some sea-touring kayaks which are fitted with bilge pumps. Kayaks and canoes can, however, be emptied in deep water if you have trained assistance from at least one other paddler. The method is known as a deep water rescue and is described on page 158.

If you capsize in deep water, not far from the bank, it is worth simply swimming to shore while towing the boat by one end. Swim on your back or side using a steady, rhythmical leg kick.

3
BASIC BOAT
CONTROL – KAYAKS

Having understood the distinction between straight-running kayaks and those which are shorter and designed for manoeuvring you can see that your choice of boat design will very much affect the range of skills which you will require in order to make it work. Fast-turning boats need constant attention to control but offer a multitude of exciting possibilities. Directional boats are reluctant to turn but cruise smoothly and cleanly for mile after mile. For flat water touring you need only an efficient forward-paddling action with a few very simple extra strokes to help with the odd moment of manoeuvring in narrow channels. For running white water, riding surf and coastal touring a wider range of techniques are available to you. Fast turns on the move and the eskimo roll are applicable only to rough water paddling and sea kayaking.

Choose the site for your first paddling experiences carefully. The following guidelines will help you pick a safe area that will give you the greatest opportunity to learn quickly:

- The water should be non-flowing, as in a lake, or at least very slow-moving, as in a canal.
- It should be sheltered from wind – the less the better.
- The banks or water's edge should be free from overhanging obstructions such as low trees or ledges which might impede your launching or landing.
- Shallow water up to about half a metre in depth is ideal. You will feel more confident knowing that it's always possible to get out and walk.

Spend some time finding the right place. You should feel comfortable there, not intimidated by the icy stare of anglers, for example, or in danger of being run over by sailboarders, Also, make certain that you aren't breaking some local by-law by going afloat in this spot. The presence of other paddlers is obviously a big help. All of this advice applies to both open canoe and kayak paddlers.

———————— Moving forwards ————————

You move a kayak along in exactly the same way that a swimmer moves through the water; i.e. you get a grip on some water and then pull yourself past it. A swimmer doing the front crawl pulls alternately left-right and that is precisely what you should do in your kayak, except you use the paddle blades as an extension of your hands. The paddling action is rhythmical and continuous like swimming or walking and you'll be surprised to find that your arms are quite receptive to this smooth action. Don't try to guide your arms, let them get on with it while you pay attention to the effect this is having on the kayak.

Kayaking, like swimming, involves gripping the water and pulling yourself through it. Your paddles make better purchase than hands but hands have the important advantage of feeling.

Think of each paddle stroke as being like grabbing a nearby post in the ground.

Figure 3.1 Kayak strokes

> **Basic guidance [the first 15 minutes]**
>
> - Sit upright and check that your grip on the paddle is equal along the length.
> - Look in the direction of travel and see the nose of the kayak pointing the way.
> - Keep the kayak moving, at a *slow* speed.
> - If the nose swings off course, even slightly, correct it by paddling on one side only.
> - As you do this, watch the nose come back on course and then go back to balanced paddling on each side.

A fast-turning kayak will swing wildly as if wanting only to travel in circles. Every beginner experiences this exasperating, out of control, feeling. You are doing nothing wrong – simply by continuing to practise, and following the steps described you will steadily learn to influence the kayak's movements more and more. If you have started in a straight-running kayak this first step will pass virtually unnoticed but you should give attention to controlling the precise direction of the boat's run.

> **Steering using the 'stern rudder'**
>
> - Get the kayak moving forwards.
> - Without changing your grip on the paddle shaft, turn slightly and trail the right blade deep in the water at the rear of the kayak, close to its edge.
> - Keep looking forwards, seeing the nose of the boat in relation to your direction of travel.
> - With your rearmost arm, pressure the blade outwards from the kayak side.
> - The nose of the kayak will swing to the right.

The stern rudder is called a *steering stroke*, but really it is simply the action of trailing a paddle blade close to the rear side (left or right) of the kayak as it runs forwards through the water. It is a very effective way to control direction as it offers little resistance to the smooth glide of the boat. Of course it only works while the boat is moving. You can use the stern rudder to help you steer a straight course by applying it every time the kayak swings off line.

Figure 3.2 Stern rudder

- Do at least ten practice runs of this, starting each time with the boat moving smoothly forwards.
- Now practise turns to the left using the stern rudder on the left.
- Once you have applied a stern rudder and the kayak has responded, what happens to the kayak's forward motion? The boat gradually loses momentum. See if you can keep the boat flowing forward by returning to normal forward paddling immediately after you have used a stern rudder.
- Switching stern rudders from side-to-side gives you very precise steering control. Try quick shifts from one to the other in the same run. What does the nose of the boat do?

Notice the position of the blade in this stroke, it is:

- Upright, like a ship's rudder
- Fully immersed, again like a ship's rudder
- Well to the rear and tucked in, close to the side

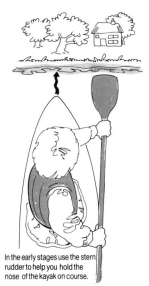

In the early stages use the stern rudder to help you hold the nose of the kayak on course.

Figure 3.3.1 Steering (I)

Set yourself some stern ruddering problems:

● Steer between two markers set to just more than the kayak's width
● Use a stern rudder to swing the boat neatly into the bank, as if you were getting out
● Paddle a wide zigzag course, stern ruddering in one direction and then paddling off. Repeat the turn in the other direction and so on

The final stage in this technique is as follows:

Basic guidance [final stage]

● Start the boat running and apply a stern rudder to the right.

● As you pressure away from the kayak side, change the pressure to pull back towards the kayak.

● This change in pressure gives you a limited amount of steering to the left. This means that you can now manoeuvre in both directions with a reasonable degree of control without necessarily having to change sides.

Remember

● The pressure which you apply to the blade is steady and prolonged, not sudden or jerky.
● The stern rudder causes a wide turn rather than a fast spin.

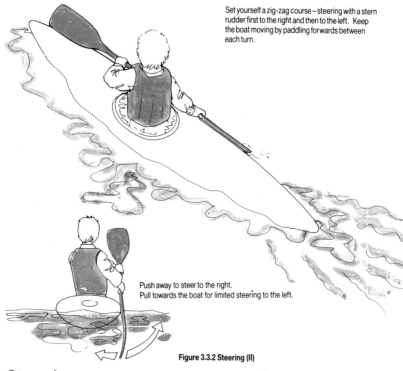

Set yourself a zig-zag course – steering with a stern rudder first to the right and then to the left. Keep the boat moving by paddling forwards between each turn.

Push away to steer to the right.
Pull towards the boat for limited steering to the left.

Figure 3.3.2 Steering (II)

Stopping

You move a kayak in reverse by placing each blade into the water behind you and pushing yourself backwards past it. If you are travelling forwards and you want to stop suddenly, you simply go into reverse.

Going into reverse
• Get the boat moving forwards at slow speed.
• Change your paddling to short reversing strokes by pushing water forwards instead of backwards.
• Pay attention to the boat's direction as it comes to a halt.
• Use quick, shallow reversing strokes to make the boat stop.

Try to control the stopping so that the kayak stays on line as you gradually apply the brakes – using a sequence of short, sharp strokes is the best way to achieve this.

Practise this lots of times until your arms are used to going from forward to reverse gear!

- Now get used to stopping the boat at higher speeds.
- Set yourself emergency stop situations, with someone shouting 'stop!'

Remember

- In an emergency stop you are bringing to rest your own weight plus that of the kayak. There is a considerable amount of momentum involved so you can expect to apply a lot of effort.
- Being able to stop quickly under control has important safety implications, so practise hard.
- Don't bother to turn the blades over – use the back of the blades for your reversing strokes.

——— Spinning the boat ———

A kayak turning like a Catherine wheel is described as *spinning*. Fast-turning kayaks do it beautifully, while those built for travelling straight are somewhat reluctant. The stroke which creates spinning is called *the sweep*. It is the key stroke in a great many paddling techniques, so you should work hard to get it right. If you have been struggling to make your boat run a straight course you will find that learning the sweep will be a big help towards taking control. By incorporating sweep strokes as you paddle forwards, you can hold the course while continuing to keep the power on.

For the moment, forget completely about travelling on a straight course. Let the kayak come to rest well clear of any obstructions.

The forward sweep

- Reach forward on your right side, without changing your grip, and with a straight right arm bury the blade in the water close to where your feet are.
- Drive the nose of the kayak away from this blade as far as it will go to the left (this is the spin).
- The blade will 'travel' in a wide arc towards the rear of the boat.
- Just before the blade meets the rear of the boat lift it out.
- Repeat this so that the kayak continues to spin.

This is called the *forward sweep*. It is a long, wide pull, with a straight arm, starting at the front and travelling to the rear. The blade should be fully immersed so that it gains maximum grip on the water. By letting your trunk follow the paddle as it sweeps you can increase the amount of power and also the range in the stroke. This turning of the shoulders from the hips is called *trunk rotation*, and it plays an important part in other aspects of kayaking technique.

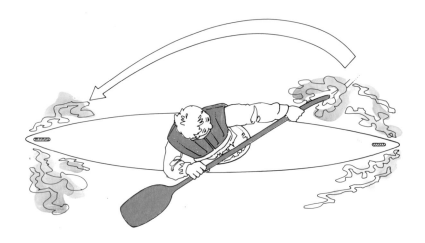

Figure 3.4 The forward sweep

- Do four consecutive sweeps to the right. Let the kayak glide through the spin as you recover the blade each time.
- Now change direction and do four sweeps on the other side. Continue, alternating the spin from one direction to the other.

Don't force the sweep stroke. It should be possible to count to three as you do one complete sweep. Pulling the blade through the water any faster amounts to wasted effort.

Now you have mastered two elements of control – you can *create* a spin and *change the direction* of a spin. The next stage is to try applying a sweep while the kayak is moving forwards.

Figure 3.5

In the sweep you grip the water with the paddle and drive the kayak away from it.

The sweep-on-the-move

- Start the boat moving slowly forwards and pay attention to the nose.

- Put a good sweep in on the left and watch the nose displace itself to the right – continue paddling.

- Put a sweep in on the right this time (keeping the pull long, wide and deep) and create a turn to the left.

This is termed the *sweep-on-the-move*. To make this work you need to be positive in your approach. When you apply a sweep you have to *want* to make it work, otherwise the kayak will remain in control and your efforts will be overpowered. In the early stages this exercise might require more than one sweep to cause the change in direction. This will most certainly be the case if you are working in a straight-running kayak.

It is the sweep-on-the-move which most paddlers use to help them steer a straight course when paddling directly from A to B. So it would work like this:

Steering a straight course

- Start the kayak moving with its nose pointing at a definite target such as a buoy, a boulder or even a tree on the bank.

- As it swings off course introduce a sweep stroke and watch closely as the nose comes back on line.

- If it over-corrects or needs more turn, simply add more sweeps.

Keep the kayak's forward speed well down while you are learning these movements. High forward speed makes corrections more diffi-cult. Once you are more confident you can work at increasing the speed.

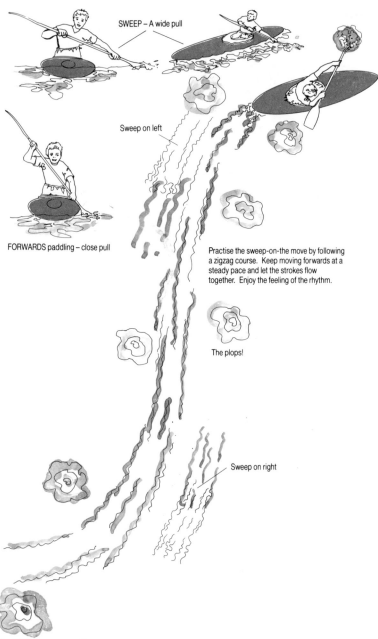

SWEEP – A wide pull

Sweep on left

FORWARDS paddling – close pull

Practise the sweep-on-the move by following a zigzag course. Keep moving forwards at a steady pace and let the strokes flow together. Enjoy the feeling of the rhythm.

The plops!

Sweep on right

Figure 3.6 The sweep-on-the-move

Now try the reverse sweep:

The reverse sweep

- Start sitting upright, with the boat stationary.

- Rotate towards one side and place the blade (fully immersed) into the water at the rear.

- Sweep towards the front in a wide arc, this time finishing at your feet.

The reverse sweep starts at the rear of the boat. The arm is straight and the blade is fully immersed.

Figure 3.7 The reverse sweep

The same principles of deep blade, straight arm and rotating trunk apply as for the forward sweep. Remember to practise the reverse sweep on both sides.

Try this exercise:

- Start with a stationary boat.
- Start the boat turning to the right with a forward sweep on the left.
- Maintain the spin by doing a reverse sweep on the right.
- Continue the right spin using alternate forward and reverse sweeps.

This is a good exercise for coordination and balance. Once you get a rhythm going you should go through a mental list checking off the correct parts of the movement as you do them. Practise in both directions.

Here is the next exercise to try:

- Paddle a straight course for about 15 metres.
- Make a turn to the left using a forward sweep on the right followed by a reverse sweep on the left.
- Paddle a straight 15 metres again.
- Make a turn to the right – forward sweep (left) followed by a reverse sweep (right).
- Keep going until you've completed 5 turns in each direction.

Getting into a flow is the aim of this exercise. Move rhythmically, applying smooth, positive and unhurried sweeps. This exercise is tiring and that's good, because it is helping you to build the specific strength and flexibility which is necessary for skilful kayak paddling.

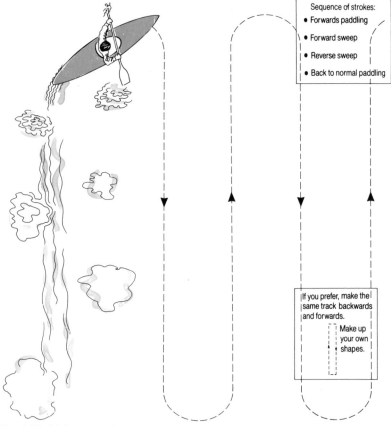

Figure 3.8 The linked sweeps exercise

Remember

- The blade is fully immersed.
- The arm is straight.
- Trunk rotation helps with the work and with the range of the movement.
- The pull is prolonged and constant, not sudden and short.

Reversing

Kayaks run easily in reverse and you have already had some experience of this from the 'stopping' practice. Going backwards is something which is done more out of necessity than out of fun, but it does provide a simple solution to some manoeuvring situations which might otherwise be rather complicated. Reversing the kayak involves pushing each blade forwards. The rear faces of the blades are used so there is no need to roll the paddles over.

Basic guidance while reversing

- Start by sitting upright with the kayak at a complete standstill.

- Start it moving backwards with short, gentle strokes.

- Look over one shoulder or, if you prefer, alternate shoulders as you paddle.

- Check your direction of travel by sighting the end of the boat against a fixed object on the bank.

- Move slowly and control minor deviations from your course with reverse sweeps.

When reversing:
- Look where you are going over each shoulder.
- Use trunk rotation
- Move the boat slowly.
- Use the back of the blades.

Figure 3.9 Reversing

Learning to reverse is necessary for:
- Stopping
- Getting out of narrow dead end channels
- Manoeuvring in white water

Reversing practice needs to be given time. It can be frustrating in the early stages but, just as with learning to reverse a car, when you really need to use it you will be glad you went to the trouble to learn. Reversing is also a good way of developing your trunk rotation and that is something which you can always afford to spend time on.

Set yourself some reversing challenges:

- A simple A to B course. See if you can do it in as straight a line as possible.
- Do some emergency stops while reversing.
- Set a reversing course around markers – a figure of eight or a triangular course, for example.

Moving sideways

Unlike most other vessels a kayak moves sideways very willingly. Getting away from a bank or moving sideways onto a raft is therefore no problem whatsoever for the kayak paddler. This lateral movement of the boat is called *sideslip* and the stroke which brings it about is called *the draw*.

Start by sitting upright, with the boat stationary and your hands in their normal position on the shaft.

The drawstroke

- Place the paddle in an upright position in the water, level with your hip.

- The blade in the water should be parallel to the boat side and should be fully immersed.

- Draw the boat up to the blade.

- Remove the blade from the water by rotating it through 90 degrees and slicing it upwards. This wrist rotation is called *wrist rolling*.

Reaching well out at the start of the draw ensures that you get the maximum sideslip travel out of a single pull. The sideslip travel can of course be kept up for as long as necessary by stringing draw strokes together. Once you have tried out the basic action of the draw stroke you will almost certainly need to work at gaining control over the direction of the sideslip. To improve your control in this area try the following:

Gaining control over the direction

- Always rotate your trunk slightly towards the direction of travel. This increases the range of movement available to you.

- Experiment with the track of the pull.

- Pull from the starting position slightly towards your feet. What effect does this have on the sideslip?

The draw requires:
- A deep blade
- The top arm across the head
- A sideslip with level boat

Steering the sideslip:
- Try altering the direction of the pull in order to control the sideslip
- The starting point is always directly out from your hip

Figure 3.10 The draw stroke

A number of key features contribute to an efficient draw, these are:

- The blade must be placed deep in the water;
- The kayak must be kept level during the sideslip (or else its edges will dig in and cause drag);
- The top arm should reach across the top of your head so that, seen from the front, the whole paddle is on the drawing side of the boat.

You can break the draw stroke down into some key parts and rehearse each separately. This gives you the opportunity to reduce the relatively complicated whole action into easily-learned components. These can then be strung together in the complete stroke. The parts to try are:

- The *top arm position*, which makes a 'window' to look through;
- The *reach out* – you can even try this sitting at the edge of the bank;
- The *wrist-roll* which is used when you come to remove the paddle from the water;

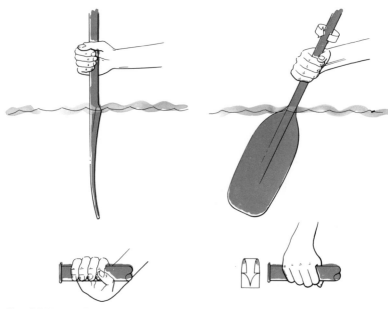

Figure 3.11 The wrist roll
To slice the blade vertically out of the water at the end of a draw, wrist roll the paddle shaft through 90 degrees. The wrist roll is like a motor-cycle twist grip action.

- The *blade recovery* – the phase of the action where you choose to return for another draw. Basically there are two ways of doing this. One is to return through the air to the starting point and the other is to leave the blade in the water and to knife it outwards through the water with the blade at 90° to the boat.

Once you have a reasonable feel for the way the draw works and you can make the boat sideslip at least roughly in the direction you choose, you need to get stuck into some serious practising. You must apply yourself to this because in the early stages draw stroke practice can be unsatisfying. It eventually pays off when you realise how important sideways movement is in kayak paddling.

Devise your own draw stroking tasks using markers or natural features on your local water. Set lots of different problems and try to gauge your improvement.

Here are a few suggestions for exercises:

- Travel in a continuous sideslip across the pond or between markers and then change direction. Try four complete crosses.
- Draw into the wind or current (remember to keep the kayak level).
- Change the direction of the sideslip every four or five draws, i.e. five draw strokes to the right followed by five to the left and so on.
- Draw on the move. Paddle forwards and introduce a sideslip by doing a single draw. Think about this one – what change do you have to make to the working blade in this version of the draw?

Keeping upright

It would be easy to think that a paddler sitting in a kayak relies purely on an acute sense of balance to keep from falling into the water. This is simply not the case. Most kayak paddlers can recover totally from being a long way off balance. It is not at all uncommon to see a canoeist in white water return to the upright after an upset where one shoulder was well below the surface. The technique which a paddler employs to restore balance is called the *recovery stroke*. It is performed as follows:

The low recovery stroke

- Sit upright in the boat with your hands in their normal grip on the paddle shaft.

- Hold the paddle at tummy level (just above the cockpit rim) with the right blade parallel to the water surface.

- Lean gently towards the water on the right and let the blade press onto the surface.

- As the blade makes contact with the water, use the resistance to snap yourself back upright.

Try this at least a dozen times, getting the feel for the support offered by the flat blade against the water. Do the same on the left-hand side. Don't throw yourself totally off balance yet – get familiar with the overall action first. Check each time that your hands remain aligned on the shaft, exactly as they would be for normal forward paddling.

Alternating the low recovery stroke

- Now try alternating, from a recovery on the right into one on the left and so on. This gets you used to finding the position quickly, by feel, rather than by having to look at the paddle each time.

A recovery stroke has to become part of your instinctive reflexes. To this end, try to think of the blades as being your hands, or if you prefer, as extensions to your hands. You already possess a perfectly good dry-land reflex whereby you reach out with a hand if you feel yourself falling over. Have you experienced this reflex in a canoe? It is very common with learners. You feel the boat overbalancing – drop the paddle – and reach for the water or maybe the canoe sides. If you can invoke that same reflex and simply substitute the paddle blade for the outstretched hand then you will have achieved a lot towards helping yourself stay upright.

Remember

- Before attempting recovery practice check that you can safely capsize and exit from your kayak. Shallow water or a heated swimming pool is the place to try this out.
- Recovery strokes need to be truly instinctive if they are to be effective – this means a lot of practice.
- Start off with gentle rocking movements and progress towards really committing yourself to the stroke.

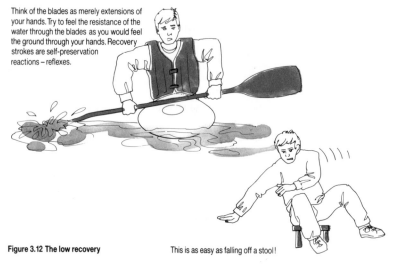

Think of the blades as merely extensions of your hands. Try to feel the resistance of the water through the blades as you would feel the ground through your hands. Recovery strokes are self-preservation reactions – reflexes.

Figure 3.12 The low recovery

This is as easy as falling off a stool!

One thing which you might have noticed with this stroke is that the blade you drive off tends to sink into the water. That is no great problem but you do have to be careful when it comes to lifting it out. It is not uncommon for a beginner to carry off a superb recovery and then promptly capsize through trying to lift a flat blade out of the water. There is a better way:

Blade lift-out

- The method is simply to let your elbow drop, wrist-roll the blade through 90 degrees and slice it vertically out of the water.

You can practise the paddle stroke and the blade lift-out phases as separate parts if you wish, but you must always get back to practising the whole action.

The stroke which is described above is more accurately known as the *low recovery stroke*. Although it can be used in any type of kayak, it is especially useful in those with open cockpits where the paddler's knees and thighs do not actively grip the boat.

It is in kayaks with cockpit arrangements involving knee or thigh braces that the paddler can recover from the most severe out-of-balance situations. In these boats the *high recovery* stroke offers greater versatility and is the one which you should try to perfect in training.

The high recovery stroke

- Start by sitting upright, with normal paddling grip.
- Hold the paddle at chest height, with your bent elbows directly below the shaft.
- Make the right blade horizontal to the water surface and drive it down onto the water as you did with the low recovery stroke.

This is the *high* recovery. Does it feel rather awkward? If it does then you are getting it right because the action only really takes shape when you are cranked over towards the water, as you would be if you lost balance.

Introducing the brace

- Prepare for the high recovery again as above but this time lean sideways towards the water and introduce the brace just before you lose balance.

What happens inside the kayak is the key to recovery strokes. By rotating at the hips the knee raises the edge. The body remains low until the final movement.

Figure 3.13.1 The high recovery

Controlling the balance of the kayak with your knees is a very important aspect of the high recovery. From being tipped onto one edge you return the boat to the level by driving upwards with your lower leg. Good solid knee or thigh contact with the inside of the kayak is essential if you are to learn effective high recoveries. The footrest should be fixed so that your legs are kept bent at the knees, which are in turn held firmly against the underside of the deck. Work on these simple exercises to get the feel of controlling boat balance:

- Set one paddle blade on a nearby shoulder-high bank. Raise the kayak onto one edge and then the other by applying pelvis rotation and knee-lift. Be sure to tilt the kayak with the hip and leg action, rather than by throwing your shoulders from one side to the other.
- Try to find a firm branch or pole which you can hold at shoulder height. Two friends holding your paddles will do. Use the support to steady yourself while you concentrate on setting the boat as far as possible onto each edge. Try to notice what parts of your body are involved in the action.

In the high recovery the paddle is retrieved from the water using the same wrist-roll and vertical slice out as was described in the low recovery, except that the rotation is in the opposite direction, i.e. the elbow moves upwards.

You might already have noticed that in the low recovery the back

The high recovery is about having your weight under the shaft, as though you were hanging from it.

Practise high recoveries with support so that you can concentrate on the hip action. You can go back to water for support afterwards.

Figure 3.13.2

face of the blade (blade faces are explained in figure 1.8, p. 17) is used to make contact with the water and in the high recovery it is the driving face. The low recovery is a downward pushing action, like pressing on a desktop as you stand up. The high recovery is a pulling or hanging action, like doing chin ups on a bar.

- Practise the high recovery by resting the paddle blade on a low bank for support and get used to applying the hip action by tilting and then levelling the boat. Concentrate on making large rolling movements of the boat and not on lifting your body weight out of the water.
- Practise alternate high recovery strokes on either side. This is a good way gradually to increase the amount of *commitment* which you make to the stroke.
- Once you have some confidence that you can prevent a real upset, get a helper to stand in the water holding the end of your kayak. Ask him or her to twist the boat enough to throw you off balance to each side and see if you can deal with it.

One final comment about the recovery stroke. If you can somehow prolong a recovery so that the support from the blade lasts for more than just an instant then you are using what is called a *brace*. Braces are possible in surfing and certain white water situations where the speed of water rushing past the blade produces a relatively continuous supporting platform.

Fast turns on the move

Low brace turn

Any kayak can be made to turn more easily as it runs forwards by tilting it towards one edge. This changes the kayak's waterline shape, helping it to trace a smooth, curving turn through the water. This effect is very noticeable in straight-running kayaks. Sitting on the level, these boats have a pronounced keel-line which holds the boat on a true course. If the boat is tilted, the keel loses its grip and is replaced by a much flatter shape which offers considerably less resistance to turning. Fast-turning kayaks also respond well to tilting on the move, and a stroke which takes advantage of this is the low brace turn.

The low brace turn is a stroke offering a high degree of stability. Although the boat is tilted, the paddler remains in balance. The paddle shaft offers a good handlebar on which to gain support.

In the low brace turn the kayak is tilted – very much as you would tilt a bicycle to go round a gentle bend.

Figure 3.14 The low brace turn

The low brace turn

- Start with the boat running straight ahead and decide which way you want to turn.

- Tip the kayak onto the edge on that side.

- At the same time place the paddle into the low recovery position on the same side and, with the leading edge of the blade raised very slightly, let it drag along with you.

- The combined effect of the dragging blade and tilted boat will create a steady gentle turn.

- As the boat slows and the turn is completed, return to the level and continue paddling.

The tilt is induced by the same hip and knee action which you used in the recovery stroke. The low brace turn works well in all types of kayaks from white water to marathon racers. Those with large, open cockpits are limited in the amount of tilt possible because of the lack of knee grip.

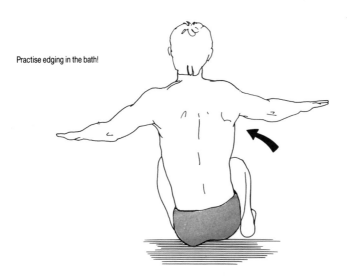

Practise edging in the bath!

The kayak is edged during the low brace turn. The edging is created from the hips – as with the recovery stroke. You sit on one buttock, and raise the other knee.

Figure 3.15 Edging

If you are trying the low brace turn in a fast-turning kayak you might notice that the boat is initially reluctant to turn to your chosen side. This is easily remedied by starting the turn off with a sweep. So if you want to make a turn to the right:

Starting with a sweep

- From forward paddling make a forward sweep on the left side.

- As the nose of the boat swings to the right, start the tilt to the right.

- Apply the low brace and let it trail.

- When you are ready to continue paddling, simply skid the blade forwards over the surface of the water and let it be the first of your forward paddling strokes.

The turn that you get with a low brace is neither fast nor sharp. It's the kind of turn you might get if the boat were on rails. The low risk and high stability of the low brace turn makes it an important stroke in the beginner's repertoire and this is the reason for its key place in the learning of white water techniques.

To help consolidate the stroke do the following exercises:

- Do a few low brace turns with the bracing blade held *close* to your side.

- Now try the turns with the bracing blade held *well away* from the side of the boat.

    Which feels more effective? It should be the second.

- This time try making a few turns using only minimal tilt.

- As above, but this time set the kayak as high on its edges as you can manage.

    Which gives the more definite turn? More tilt works best.

Now do the following exercise:

- Paddle a straight course for about 15 metres and make a low brace turn to the right. Use this stroke sequence: forward paddling; forward sweep; low brace turn. Do the same again, making a turn to the left. Each turn should take you through well over 90 degrees. Do at least ten turns, have a rest, and then repeat the exercise twice more. Work at slow speeds

This exercise helps you to develop *flow*, i.e. the smooth linking of all the different actions involved. When your paddling flows, the strokes cease to feel and look like unconnected parts and the boat movement takes on a mysterious energy which is a delight to experience.

Remember that the low brace turn does not require you to place a great deal of your body weight on the trailing blade. The boat tilt (or *edging* as it is more properly called) is achieved by raising one buttock and shifting your centre of balance over the other. Edging is a result of delicate weight re-alignment and not throwing the trunk wildly out to one side.

The bow rudder

Of all the turning strokes in kayaking *the bow rudder* is the one which offers the paddler the greatest range of boat movements. It is a stroke which can deliver a fast, snappy spin or a long curvy turn. What is more, a bow rudder can inject speed into the kayak or alternatively cause it to slow down and stall. It is a magnificent stroke and an attacking one, ideal for the kind of positive boat control needed on rough water.

As with all other strokes, you should learn this stroke first on flat water, starting at slow speeds and working up to faster turns as your confidence grows. Start by simply getting used to the body orientation, arm position and blade angle:

The bow rudder

- From a still boat, rotate to your right, and place the right blade in the water in the position it would be in at the finish of a draw stroke.

- Take the blade forward until it is level with your knee.

- Roll both wrists down so that the blade opens a few degrees to form a V with the side of the kayak.

This is the basic bow rudder position. Your top arm should be across the top of your forehead, the shaft should be close to the vertical and the blade should be fully immersed. If the boat were to move forward now you would feel the blade grip the water and the kayak nose would be drawn around to the right. Practise moving into this position. Notice how much both wrists have to flex to get that angle on the blade. The wrist movement is exactly that which would accelerate a motor bike using the twist-grip.

The paddle shaft is a pivot around which you drive the boat. Used in fast white water, the bow rudder will turn a boat.

Always start the boat turning with a forward sweep (especially on flat water). Keep the bow rudder on until you have as much turn as you require.

The narrow V formed by the bow rudder blade and the side of the boat.

The bow rudder is ready and waiting to be converted into a forward power stroke. You need only roll the wrists slightly and pull.

Figure 3.16 The bow rudder

Now try this one.

- Start the kayak on a slow run.
- Put in a sweep on the left to start a turn to the right.
- Plant the bow rudder (right) – be purposeful, make the blade bite.
- Try a few more turns but try to get your top hand (left) well across to the right side of the boat. Make only the finest of angles with the blade in the water. You will notice that if you form a wide angle the blade catches hard and is difficult to hold in place. The resulting turn is jerky and unsatisfying. Experiment with this angle until you find what feels best.
- You should now start again with the left-hand bow rudder and repeat these exercises.

Don't worry if the stroke still feels very rough and awkward after your first practice session with it. You will need to return to it several times during your training sessions before it feels really comfortable.

Using a bow rudder is a bit like running along the street, catching hold of a lamp post and spinning around it. The paddle blade is locked solidly into the water while you hang onto the shaft. Because you have the extra encumbrance of a kayak attached to your hips and legs you must consciously drive the boat around the turn. This feeling of *driving the kayak around the paddle shaft* is a good one. Your feet on the footrest and knees in the braces provide the grip on the boat – think of driving your legs and feet around the turn.

The paddle position in the bow rudder is not a static one. The truth is that, apart from the basic starting position, the angle and orientation of the blade change a great deal, according to the type of turn you want to make. Have a look at how the bow rudder can be easily converted to forward paddling:

Converting bow rudder to forward paddling

- The aim is to bow rudder, turn and then go directly into a forward paddling stroke without removing the blade from the water.
- Start the boat running and apply a sweep followed by a bow rudder (on the opposite side).
- At the end of the turn rotate the blade to parallel to the boat and slice it forwards through the water.
- Wrist-roll the blade inwards so that it becomes the start of a forward paddling stroke and pull straight through.

This sounds much more complicated than it is in practice and it gives a beautifully smooth and efficient action which keeps the boat moving forward. Set up this exercise for yourself:

● Place two markers (floats or posts of some kind) about 15 to 20 metres apart. Improvised buoys can be made by placing a ball into a plastic carrier bag and closing the neck with string. The string can be tied to a brick or simple weight, which will anchor the buoy to the bottom. Paddle a figure of eight course around the markers using the following stroke sequence – forward paddling; sweep; bow rudder and slice to forward paddling. Alternate your turns to the right and to the left.

Things to aim for in this exercise are:

● To keep the boat moving forward all the time;
● To maintain a constant boat speed through the water (about 50% of your maximum);
● To do at least four complete circuits, rest and then another four;
● Flow.

In this next exercise, try to visualise the boat's track through the water, very much as a lone snow skier would leave an imprint on new snow. Use one of your markers to give you a reference point around which to turn. Have a starting point at least 15 metres away from the marker.

● Approach the marker on a straight course and make a wide, curving turn which keeps you wide of the marker. The track you would leave is a very wide V with a rounded bottom.
● Approach the marker on a straight course, passing close to it. Make a sharp spin and take off in a new direction. The track is a narrow V with a point.

Repeat these exercises until you have had at least four attempts at each on both right and left sides. Take your time and go back to the same starting point for each run. See the track on the water before you start each attempt.

Now do the turns again and ask yourself these questions:

● What happens to the boat's forward speed in the tight turn and how does it change in the wide turn?
● What is the position and angle of the bow rudder blade in the tight turn and how does it change in the wide turn?

Remember

With the bow rudder:

- Trunk rotate towards the direction of the turn *before* you plant the blade
- Top arm high, forming a 'window' around your face
- Deep blade
- Drive the boat around the turn using knee and foot pressure
- Go straight into forward paddling after the turn by slicing the blade forward and wrist-rolling
- A bow rudder needs commitment – holding back makes it more difficult for you to achieve.

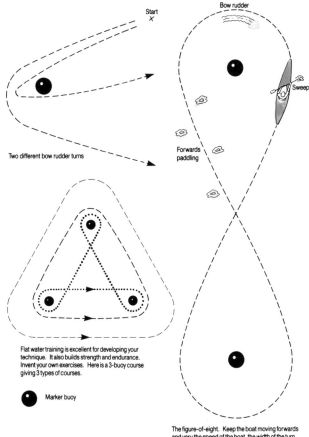

Start
×

Bow rudder

Sweep

Two different bow rudder turns

Forwards
paddling

Flat water training is excellent for developing your
technique. It also builds strength and endurance.
Invent your own exercises. Here is a 3-buoy course
giving 3 types of courses.

Marker buoy

The figure-of-eight. Keep the boat moving forwards
and vary the speed of the boat, the width of the turn
and the distance between the buoys.

Figure 3.17 The bow rudder

The eskimo roll

It is certainly not essential to learn to eskimo roll and indeed those kayaks which have large open cockpits offering no positive knee grip are mostly impossible to roll. To the white water paddler or sea tourer, however, rolling is a very important safety technique – one which can turn a capsize from being a potentially threatening situation into nothing more than an interesting incident. The paddler who can recover from a capsize by rolling back upright is more confident and more effective because he or she is achieving virtually total self-reliance. Being able to make your own decisions, take control of yourself and your boat and deal with your own problems is central to the spirit of canoeing.

An eskimo roll begins when you find yourself upside down in the water. From this inverted position you manoeuvre the paddle into a position from which you can apply a high recovery stroke and the associated hip and knee action. As a result, you pop upright again.

The roll is not difficult to learn, but it does need to be broken down into simple steps. You will be surprised how quickly you can make progress but don't worry if success isn't instant – everyone learns at his or her own rate.

If possible, try to get someone to stand in the water with you while you are learning the roll. This helps in two ways; they can act as a lifeguard and can also be your eyes, giving you important feedback so that you know if what you are *actually* doing differs from what you are *intending* to do.

Try to get access to a heated swimming pool or, if this is not possible, work at the edge of shallow water (where you can touch the bottom easily from being upside down in the kayak). Use a wetsuit if you have to work in cold water. A nose clip and also some goggles or a face mask are useful aids when you are learning the roll. It is of course necessary to wear a spray deck when doing any eskimo rolling drills. The steps are as follows.

Step 1: Familiarisation

Get used to being upside down in the kayak. Try to relax and develop your breath-holding.

Familiarisation with the underwater world

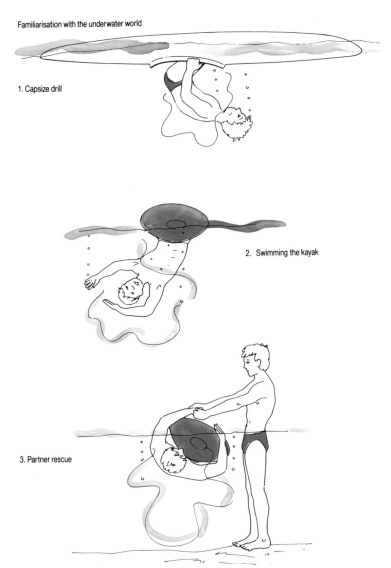

1. Capsize drill

2. Swimming the kayak

3. Partner rescue

Figure 3.18 Eskimo rolling

1

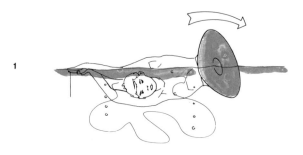

2

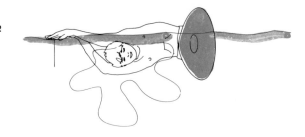

3

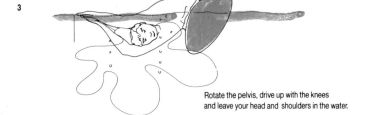

Rotate the pelvis, drive up with the knees
and leave your head and shoulders in the water.

Figure 3.19 Developing the hip action

Familiarisation

- From upright, reach under the water and grip the hull. Take a deep breath and capsize. Once you are upside down and stable, calmly remove the spray deck, place your hands behind you and come out leaning forwards.

- Repeat as above but this time tap out ten seconds with your fingers on the hull before you release the spray deck and come out. Can you reach 30 seconds? Remain relaxed and try to exit slowly.

- Capsize and see if you can swim your head to the surface (use goggles if you like). A competent person can swim a kayak the length of a swimming pool like this, lifting the head every now and then to take a breath.

- Capsize and lean forward, nose on the deck, and 'hug the boat' with your arms. Remain in that position while your partner reaches across the kayak to grip the furthest arm and roll you and the kayak upright. This 'partner rescue' allows you to stay in the boat during your learning of rolling technique. To signal to your partner for this rescue, simply bang twice on the hull of the boat.

Step 2: The hip action

You must learn to roll the boat upright by a vigorous twisting of your hips. This hip action causes the boat to roll up, leaving your head and body behind in the water. You will need a low handrail or solid bank close to water level to hold on to. One way to do this is to get your partner to hold the paddle shaft firmly at water level in a wide grip.

The hip action

- Hold the rail firmly, alongside your hip.

- Lower the near shoulder slowly into the water keeping your head above the water. Keep the boat close to the rail.

- In a single action, flick the kayak upright using knee pressure and hip rotation.

- Leave your head and shoulders close to the water – they should barely move.

It is the flick upright which is the main focus of this exercise. You should pull the boat *slowly* onto its edge and flick it *quickly* back to the level. When your hip action is correct you will notice a distinctively 'light' feel to the rolling action. If it feels strenuous and becomes a struggle, you must return to improving your hip action.

- Now lower yourself deeper into the water, again slowly, and apply the hip action to right the boat (use the mask or nose clip as your face will be just below the surface at this stage).

Keep searching for the hip rotation, leaving your head and shoulders low in the water.

- Try the same exercise as above with only the near hand gripping the rail.

This exercise is an important test of your technique. If the hip action is good, the one-handed grip should easily offer enough purchase. If you have been using brute force, it won't.

Step 3: Introducing the paddle

Introducing the paddle

- Hold one end of your paddle by the blade and shaft.
- Rest the other blade, horizontally, in your partner's hands or on solid ground close to water level.
- Get your weight close to the water surface and roll the boat onto its edge slowly. Flick it upright.

Keep the blade which you are holding in front of your face throughout this exercise.

- Keep working at this until you can recover from being completely upside down. You might find it helpful to lie back slightly as you apply the hip action. If you struggle with this go back one step for some more work on the pure hip action.
- Get your partner to remove the support from the blade by letting go after the initial stage of your pull. You should start to feel the blade grip the water in the same way as it did in the recovery stroke.
- If you don't have a partner, simply practise high recovery strokes with this elongated paddle grip. Start gently and work up to committing yourself totally to the blade.
- Do the high recovery exercise described above, trying to let the blade remain on the surface as you go over and then applying the lightest of pressure downwards as you roll up.

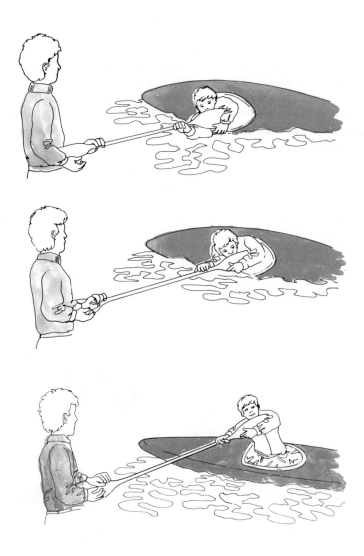

Figure 3.20 Introducing the paddle

Try not to get worried or disheartened if your efforts appear to result in failure. Give everything at least six attempts before moving to another exercise. Learning tends to follow a pattern of surges with plateaux in between – things suddenly click into place with no warning. It pays to persist, but on the other hand don't exhaust yourself totally. It is better to leave it for a while and return when you have rested than to push on past your fatigue threshold.

Step 4: 'Cueing' the paddle

When rolling 'for real' you are unlikely to have the luxury of seeing what you are doing – setting up will be done purely by feel. The starting position is therefore very important to the process because it acts as a *cue* to the sequence of actions which follow. Experienced paddlers know that time spent getting into the right starting position before attempting a roll is crucial to the ultimate success of the roll. You should first rehearse this cueing position while the kayak is upright:

Figure 3.21 Cueing the paddle

Cueing the paddle

- Hold the paddle in the 'snooker cue' grip on the deck in front of you, gripping firmly.

- Bend forward at the hips.

- The forward blade should be horizontal.

- Take the whole paddle off the deck and place it to the side, on the surface of the water. This is your starting or cue position.

Familiarise yourself with this position so that you can easily take it up in the dark.

- Now try the cueing position underwater. Set up on the surface. Capsize and, when the boat has stabilized, check the position.

    Use goggles to see how it looks and ask your partner to check from above. In your first attempt the paddle may wander out of position during the capsize – counter this by bracing it against the boat side as you flip. Once you are over and reasonably happy, use the partner rescue to return to the surface or pull up on a rail.

- This time as you cue underwater, crank yourself towards the surface and get the whole paddle shaft clear of the water. This is a simple, but important and final readying position before you roll up. Get your partner to confirm that the paddle is well clear of the surface.

Underwater – the cueing position takes the whole paddle clear of the surface.

Figure 3.22

Step 5: The sweep and strike

> **The sweep and strike**
>
> - From the position at the end of the last step take the paddle across the water surface in a wide sweep.
>
> - When it gets to about 90 degrees apply the hip action and maintain the sweep to the rear.
>
> - Lean backwards slightly as the boat rolls up and you finish back on the surface.

Make no effort to raise your trunk out of the water during the roll. As the kayak comes upright it scoops your body up with it. Only the sweep and strong hip action should be the focus of your attention.

When you succeed, you will feel confused about what actually went on. Because of the effects of disorientation, your memory won't be able to make sense of what you have just done. The secret is not to try to understand at this stage, just let it happen! As you become more confident and familiar with rolling, you will develop a clearer picture of what goes on.

A few things to remember at the beginning of each attempt:

- Before you capsize take time to fill your lungs with air. This might sound rather unnecessary to say but taking really full-capacity breaths takes conscious effort.
- If you have had a previously successful attempt, recall how that felt.
- Pause underwater to let the boat stabilise and to give yourself time to check the cue position.
- Do not try to roll until you can feel the paddle rise into the air.
- The first 90 degrees of the sweep is done with the paddle unweighted (you can take it through the air if you like). You roll on the second half.

If you are experiencing such disorientation that you cannot work out which way to sweep the paddle it is helpful to get your partner to guide it in the right direction for you. This should solve the problem and you should soon be able to sweep unassisted.

You will probably discover that you have a preferred side on which to roll. That is fine – work on this side until you get some success. If you are failing constantly with the roll, simply go back through the steps until you reach a point where you are succeeding.

It may help to get a partner to help by supporting and guiding the blade end.
Work towards doing it unaided.

Figure 3.23 Sweep and strike

Once you have achieved step 5 with some degree of certainty your next objective is to be able to roll with your hands in the normal paddling grip as opposed to the extended one.

Rolling with hands in normal grip

- From the extended grip change from holding the blade to gripping the blade/shaft joint. The other hand will move along the shaft a corresponding distance. Try a few recovery strokes and then go for a roll. Remember to take time and care over cueing.

- Continue to change the grip a few inches at a time until you are rolling with the normal, balanced hand positions.

Figure 3.24 Rolling using your normal paddling grip

4

BASIC BOAT
—— CONTROL–THE ——
OPEN CANOE

An open canoe is just as easy to learn to control as a kayak. In fact the open canoe paddle is even simpler to operate and virtually speaks for itself. All open canoes may be paddled either by a pair or a solo paddler – that's one of the reasons why they are so much fun to use. On the whole, two inexperienced paddlers in an open canoe can make progress faster than an inexperienced solo paddler – steering is easier and holding a straight course can be achieved within minutes of getting into the boat. This is all OK if you intend to have only a one-off encounter with canoeing, but if you really want to appreciate the full potential of this magnificent machine, it's worth learning a few basic skills. To do this it's best to begin as a solo paddler. Once you've developed some canoe handling skills on your own and acquired a sense of *feel* for the paddle you can easily adapt what you've learned to doubles paddling.

First of all, read the guidelines on page 55 about choosing the best place to start learning: they apply to both canoes and kayaks.

—————— The paddling position ——————

Position yourself in the middle of the canoe, facing the rear. (Most open canoes have two seats, a front and a rear. When paddling solo it is normal to use the front seat but facing the rear of the boat because the weight distribution is better in this position. In effect the solo paddler is propelling the canoe stern first.) Get on your knees towards one side of the boat, the side you feel most comfortable doing the paddling on. The canoe is slightly *heeled* to that side. This is exactly right, it puts you and your paddle within comfortable reaching distance of the water. Try this position on dry land at first. Get used to sitting on your heels and use a pad under your knees if you find the contact with the boat at all uncomfortable.

If you find kneeling too uncomfortable or even if you just want a change, simply slip back and onto the seat behind you. (Now you can see why you face the rear – it is the front seat which is closest to the centre of the boat.) The kneeling position is something you have to grow into.

—— Paddling forwards using the —— J stroke

A canoe will start to respond as soon as you exert even the slightest pressure on the water with the paddle. Keep your top hand (the one on the T grip) high so that the paddle goes in close to the side of the canoe. You will instantly notice that, as well as running forwards, the canoe also turns away from the paddle. You keep the canoe running straight, not by changing sides with the paddle, but by using a technique known as the *J stroke*. This technique contains two components, a forward-driving phase and a steering phase.

The J Stroke

- Begin the stroke by reaching forward and catching hold of the water with the blade.

- Pull past your hip with the blade. Look to the front of the boat to see it drive forwards and see the beginnings of the turn you want to cancel out.

- As the blade passes your hip, roll it through 90 degrees by twisting your top hand (as though turning a screw top lid on a jar).

- Now press the paddle shaft against the canoe side and use it to lever the blade outwards. This outwards pressure against the water swings the nose of the canoe back onto a straight course.

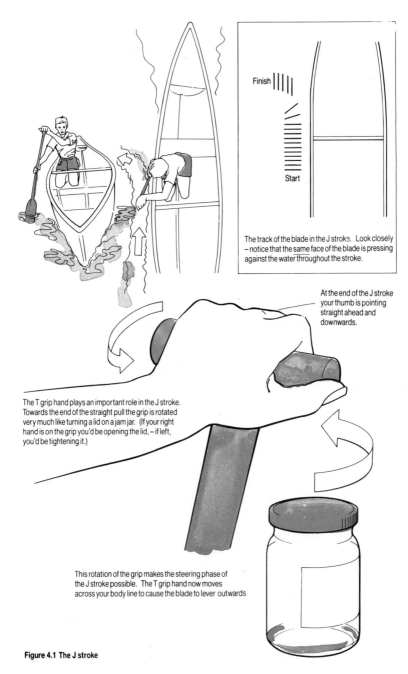

The track of the blade in the J stroke. Look closely – notice that the same face of the blade is pressing against the water throughout the stroke.

Finish

Start

At the end of the J stroke your thumb is pointing straight ahead and downwards.

The T grip hand plays an important role in the J stroke. Towards the end of the straight pull the grip is rotated very much like turning a lid on a jam jar. (If your right hand is on the grip you'd be opening the lid, – if left, you'd be tightening it.)

This rotation of the grip makes the steering phase of the J stroke possible. The T grip hand now moves across your body line to cause the blade to lever outwards

Figure 4.1 The J stroke

Remember

- The J stroke always feels very awkward at first, but you soon get so used to it you won't know it's happening.
- Use a couple of short, quick power strokes to get the boat running before you start applying J strokes.
- Keep the blade close to the side of the boat as you pull past your hip.
- Keep your T grip hand well across the boat on the same side as the paddle.
- Try to find a calm area of water, free from wind, before starting your practice.
- The J stroke is the universal method for propelling an open canoe. It should become as familiar to you as walking.

One very useful thing you can do to get the feel of the J stroke is to find a low, square-sided piece of bank beside deep water and practise the stroke kneeling on the bank. It's best if the bank is wooden so it won't damage your paddle shaft.

———— Turning on the spot ————

Most open canoes are designed for touring and so they are not difficult to hold on a straight course once you have mastered the J stroke. Turning a canoe is achieved in very much the same way as in a kayak. The sweep stroke is the key, so it's an important first technique to master.

The forward sweep, as for its kayaking namesake, resembles a normal forwards power stroke except that the pull is made in a wide arc, as far away from the canoe side as your arms will permit. Try it: you'll find that your lower arm is straight and that it is helpful to let your trunk rotate as you make the pull.

The reverse sweep applies the same principle except the starting point is at the rear and you carry the blade towards the front.

Now let's look at some manoeuvres. (The directions are for a person paddling on the right-hand side. If you prefer to paddle left-sided then switch the terms around.)

- Point the front of the boat at a marker on the water or bank and paddle a straight course to it using as much pressure in each of your J strokes as is necessary to stay on course.

- With the canoe stationary, start it turning to the left by using forward sweep strokes. Keep it spinning like this for a while so you can get used to the amount of pressure needed.
- Now spin the canoe to the right using reverse sweeps. It will slip backwards a little as well as turning, but that's to be expected.

——————— Turning on the move ———————

There are a number of ways of turning the canoe as it runs, the simplest of which are shown below. The first gives a turn away from the paddling side and the second gives what is called an *inside turn*, i.e. towards the paddle side.

Turning on the move

- Get the canoe moving forwards and turn to the left using forward sweeps.

- Again with the canoe moving forwards, turn it to the right. Do this turn, not by using reverse sweeps, but by hanging on to the steering phase of a succession of J strokes. In other words, each time you make the J prolong the lateral pressure at the end of the stroke, so that the front of the canoe turns a little to your right. This gives you a fairly wide but effective turn to your paddle side.

Both the above turns are rather wide and gentle. They are useful when you want to keep the canoe moving forwards, as well as making it turn. You can make much more snappy turns by using a stroke called *the bow cut*. If you have kayak paddling skills you will recognise the bow cut as being almost identical to the bow rudder. Remember that although the turn is faster there is a significant slowing effect on forward speed.

The bow cut

- Start the canoe moving forwards.

- Keeping your T grip hand high, reach forwards and plant the blade into the water so that its driving face forms a narrow V with the canoe side.

- Hold the blade firmly in place and let the pressure of the water against the driving face pull the canoe around to the right.

You'll certainly feel a little tippy at first but once again you'll be amazed at the way practice will help you smooth things out. The bow cut gives an inside turn, i.e. towards the paddle side. Guess how you use a bow cut to make a turn in the other direction?

The answer is the *cross bow cut*, which involves taking the blade across the canoe and placing it in the water on the other side.

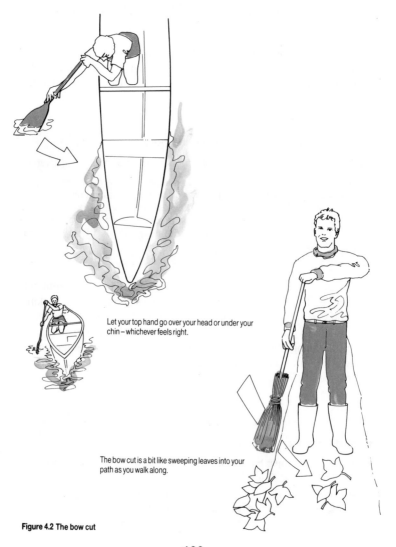

Let your top hand go over your head or under your chin – whichever feels right.

The bow cut is a bit like sweeping leaves into your path as you walk along.

Figure 4.2 The bow cut

—————— Moving sideways ——————

Sideways movement (sideslip) is created by using the *draw stroke* (towards the paddle side) and the *pry stroke* (away from the paddle side).

The draw stroke

- Place the paddle into the water on the right side so the blade is aligned parallel with the canoe side.

- Keeping your top hand high pull the canoe across the water towards the blade.

- Just before the canoe and blade meet rotate the paddle through 90 degrees by rolling your wrists and slice it outwards.

- Repeat the draw if more sideslip is needed.

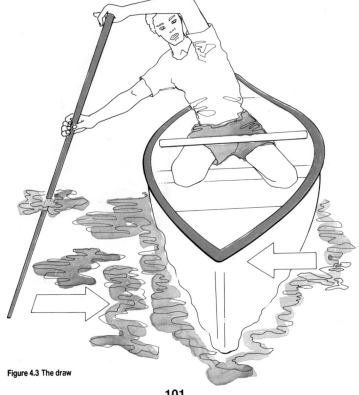

Figure 4.3 The draw

Notice that the lower hand is holding the paddle shaft against the canoe. This is the pivot point for the lever.

The pry is like moving the canoe along a ladder by levering off the rungs with a pole.

Figure 4.4 The pry

The pry stroke

- Place the paddle well into the water with the blade aligned parallel with the canoe side. The paddle should be vertical, with your top hand somewhere around head height.

- Hold the paddle shaft against the canoe side with your lower hand.

- Work your top hand to lever the blade against the water, using the canoe side as the pivot point.

- Each lever stroke should be short and hard. The paddle is rotated through 90 degrees and slices back into the canoe side between each lever stroke.

The pry feels particularly odd at first and you might well wonder if you're making any impression at all. It takes a while to get the feel of levering against the water and you should concentrate on trying to get this feeling. Imagine your canoe is sitting balanced across a ladder – now pry your way along it by hooking the tip of the paddle into the rungs and levering against the side of the canoe. That's the basis upon which the pry stroke works.

Remember

- You achieve sideslip by lots of *short* jabbing strokes rather than one long stroke.
- Always start with the paddle vertical or even with the T grip end sloped towards the direction of travel.
- It's a smooth back and forth action of your top hand.

———— Staying upright ————

An open canoe is a very stable craft and on all but the roughest water you are unlikely to feel threatened by a capsize. If you do need to steady yourself for any reason you should use a *brace*. This means resting the blade on the surface of the water and using it as a kind of handrail.

The brace

- Hold the paddle across your stomach with your knuckles pointing down.

- Extend the paddle to the side and rest the blade on the water surface.

- Feel the firm support that you get from it by pressing down with the hand nearest the blade.

You can use a brace to give you quick support, say if you unexpectedly hit an underwater object, or it can be trailed along the surface to give reassurance when you simply feel a little unsteady.

One thing which you might wonder about is what happens if you need to brace on the side you aren't paddling on. Well, firstly, you are much less likely to need this because your weight is already on the opposite side. Secondly, you will learn to anticipate destabilising forces from this direction and place more weight on the paddling side.

Figure 4.5 The brace

Reversing

Getting the boat moving in reverse is virtually self-explanatory but you do have to think about steering. The reversing strokes make the canoe turn away from the paddle, so you need to build in something which counteracts this. The reverse J is the stroke which you should use.

The reverse J stroke

- Start the canoe moving by twisting around and pulling the water towards you with a few short strokes (see figure 4.6).

- Now carry the blade past you in a reversing stroke (leading with the back of the blade).

- As you come to the limit of your reach roll the paddle through 90 degrees and pry off the side of the canoe. This brings the boat back on course.

If you need to turn away from the paddle side while reversing, simply change to reverse sweep strokes.

Start the canoe running in reverse by twisting around and pulling water towards you.

At the end of a normal reversing stroke swivel the paddle into a pry. This gives you steering control. The whole thing is called the Reverse J.

Figure 4.6 The reverse J

5

HANDLING
WHITE WATER

The purpose of this section is to give you a clear picture of the kinds of things you need to *know* and the things you need to be able to *do* in order to handle simple white water safely. As is the case throughout this book, your safety comes first when you set about preparing your own learning.

The starting point for learning white water paddling skills has got to be based on sound basic boat control. If you haven't already done so, you should give serious attention to the preceding chapters on building your basic skills. Remember, basic stroke practice should be on *non-moving water* until you can totally control the direction of the boat as it runs. Very slow-moving water such as canals would also be suitable for this. Faster flowing water, such as you get in rivers or tideways, however, takes you into a new league. Don't be frightened to move on to teaching yourself moving water techniques but do be extremely cautious.

This section is written mainly with the kayak paddler in mind because it is, in my opinion, the more suitable craft for the beginner in rough water. The principles and guidelines, however, still apply to the open canoe which can most definitely cope with white water.

The first thing you must appreciate about flowing water, or *current*, is that it is unrelenting and powerful, however innocuous its appearance. When you are afloat on a current it will carry you along. Unless you actively take charge, the river will only too willingly decide where you go. Maybe it's obvious, but if you stop paddling while in a current, you definitely *do not* stop moving. You will notice that I speak of *flowing* and *moving* water under the one broad heading of *white* water. As far as the paddler is concerned they both need to be treated the same way.

—————— How and where to learn ——————

If at all possible, try to learn moving water techniques in the presence of at least one other paddler. This makes good safety sense. It is very likely that you will take at least one capsize during this period and a friend in a kayak can be a big help. Someone with instructional experience will know how best to help but a fellow learner can soon work something out.

Here are some guidelines to getting organised for learning rough water paddling:

- Choose the right location. Use a piece of water where the flow is visible, clearly defined and not in full flood. There should be no weirs around or trees in the flow. (See under *Hazards* in this section).
- Have the correct equipment organised before you start (see below).
- Be practised and confident at getting out of your kayak in the event of capsize *and* learn to eskimo roll.
- Spend time studying the current from the bank *before* you get afloat – it's not easy to see from the water.

◢ *Equipment and boat*

To do anything other than very rudimentary rough water paddling you will need a *closed cockpit* kayak. This means you will be able to grip the boat with your knees and thighs. A (correctly adjusted) footrest and maximum internal flotation will be essential. Use front and rear air bags to increase the (manufacturer's) standard flotation and tie them in. Ensure that all air bag inflation tubes are tucked well out of the way from your feet and seat area; there should be no string or rope lying loose in the cockpit. Check also that your end grabs are both in good shape.

You must also have a helmet, spray deck and buoyancy aid. In winter use a wetsuit, warm underclothing and a canoe cag. Remember to carry a sponge to help keep the boat dry inside.

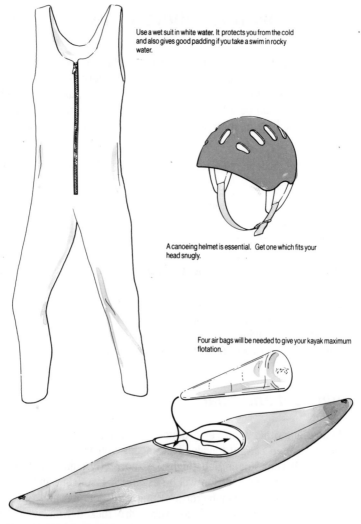

Use a wet suit in white water. It protects you from the cold and also gives good padding if you take a swim in rocky water.

A canoeing helmet is essential. Get one which fits your head snugly.

Four air bags will be needed to give your kayak maximum flotation.

Figure 5.1 Additional equipment for white water

'Reading' the current

To become a rough water paddler and to enjoy it to the fullest, you must learn the language of the river. This means recognising the formations which appear on the surface and understanding the implications they have for the paddler.

Flow variation

The surface rate of flow across a straight stretch of river is not even. It is fastest in the middle and slower, because of friction, at the edges. Float a twig downstream and prove this to yourself.

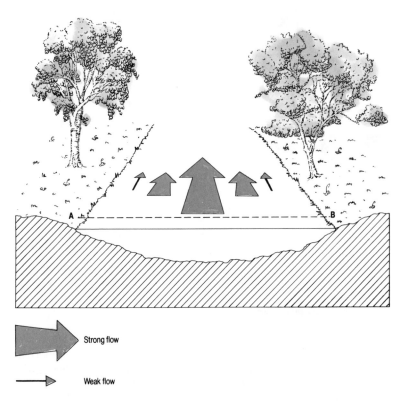

Strong flow

Weak flow

Figure 5.2 Flow variation

What happens at a bend?

On a bend the strongest flow travels to the outside of the curve. The rate is progressively weaker towards the inside of the bend.

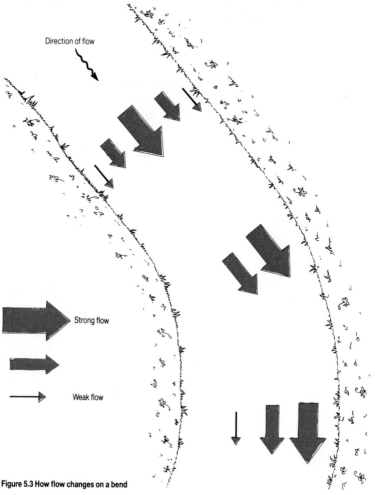

Direction of flow

Strong flow

Weak flow

Figure 5.3 How flow changes on a bend

The V-sign rule!

The V-sign rule is the way the river tells you about two important changes in the flow. Watch out for subtle (or obvious) shading of the water in the form of Vs. These are cues which help you to begin to 'read' white water.

Where there is an acceleration of flow a *downstream V* is seen (the V points in the direction of the flow). This may be caused by water being squeezed between obstructions such as rocks or bridge piers. For one reason or another the flowing water has been concentrated and paddlers look for downstream Vs because they indicate the main, deep-water channel which is to be followed.

Direction of flow

Figure 5.4 Downstream V

Isolated underwater obstructions (and indeed surface obstructions), show themselves in the form of *upstream Vs* (the V points towards the oncoming flow). You could describe running rapids in kayak or canoe as essentially following the downstream Vs and avoiding the upstream ones. Things get interesting when there are many Vs to choose from and the route through has to be inspected from the shore, memorised and then negotiated for real.

Direction of flow

Figure 5.5 Upstream V

Eddies

Paddlers use the term *eddy* to describe any piece of water which is sheltered from the main flow by some kind of obstruction. A boulder sticking out of the water in mid-channel will have an eddy on its downstream side. Look again at the upstream and downstream V diagram – can you spot the eddies?

To the white water paddler, eddies are like car parks. They are places to begin and end journeys, and also to take a rest as you pass along. The borders, where the eddy water and the flow meet, are called the *eddy lines*. Remember that eddies form at the banks as well as in midstream; good paddlers are quick to spot eddy lines which lie ahead, because as you will soon see they play an important part in manoeuvring the boat.

Always try to find a bankside eddy to put your boat onto when getting afloat and similarly when you get off the water. The bigger the eddy, the better it is. This saves you from having to hold the boat against the flow as you wriggle into or out of the cockpit. Also you will need both hands free to get your spraydeck on. Have your paddle draped across the cockpit while you do this.

Waves

Waves form in the current wherever there is a sudden increase in the rate of flow. There are two main categories of waves. The first occurs in powerful downstream Vs, where a procession of waves usually appear along the length of the narrow end of the V. These are called *standing waves*. In very strong flows they are breaking and cascading on their tops and give paddlers a good roller coaster ride as they pass over them.

The second type of wave forms when the current pours over an obstruction such as a rock or weir. This time a curling wave appears which is constantly tumbling back on itself. This wave is known to paddlers as a *stopper*. It is characterised by surface water returning upstream into a slot. When you try to pass through it you will feel the wave trying to stop you. Some stoppers are no problem and can be good fun, but others, like those which form at the base of some weirs, are literally deadly.

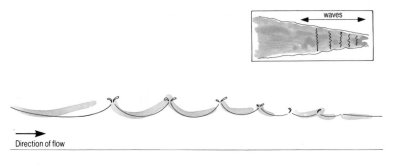

Standing waves   As they would be seen looking from the bank

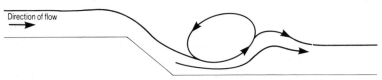

Stopper
The water movement where water pours over the edge of a weir.

Figure 5.6

◩ *Rapids*

White water is made up of stretches of rapids, and rapids are in turn made up of Vs, eddies, stoppers and waves. Boulder fields, ledges, gorges and even waterfalls are the terrain where rapids are formed and these can be enjoyed by the paddler on rivers of all scales, from the mountain stream to the mature, lowland river.

Obviously rapids vary enormously in the degree of difficulty involved in running them. This is represented by a grading system which has a scale of 1 through to 6. Grade 1 is a simple flow through shallows, and Grade 6 is a series of life-threatening stoppers and falls which require exceptional skill to negotiate successfully. Guidebooks are available which cover almost all white water rivers and these contain information on grades and access points.

The simplest rapid and the one which you should start on is one which has a single, broad, downstream V. This simple formation offers lots of technique-training possibilities and is safe, providing simple water lies immediately downstream. Once you have developed some basic techniques in this you can start tackling simple rapids with multiple Vs.

—— **White water basic technique** ——

◩ *Positive thinking*

White water technique demands commitment. When you are learning, hard, positive paddling, verging on aggression, gives better results than a gentle, timid approach.

◩ *Entering the current*

Always put your boat onto the water in an eddy (or at least slack water at the bank) with the bow facing upstream. Once you have paddled around and warmed up take up the starting position for the *break in*. The aim of this manoeuvre is to leave the eddy, cross the eddy line and enter the current so that you can carry on downstream. As you sit in the eddy facing the oncoming current, you are looking *upstream*. Behind you, in the direction of the flow, is *downstream*.

The break in

- Use fast strokes to gather forward speed towards the eddy line, aiming to cross it at about 45 degrees.

- Just before you hit the eddy line make a forward sweep which starts the boat turning downstream and at the same time raise the upstream edge of the kayak.

- Use a low brace turn on the downstream side as you enter the current and hold this as the nose gets pulled around to face downstream.

- Once the whole boat has entered the current and turned, return it to the level and paddle off.

The edging is important – if you don't edge you might well be overbalanced as you enter the flow. Once you get slick at the break in, start using a bow rudder with the blade driven into the current, instead of the low brace.

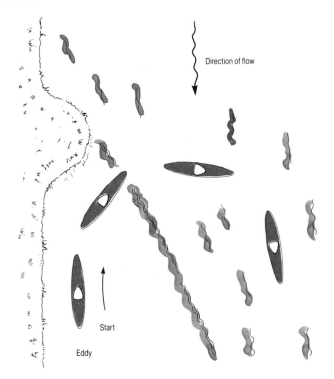

figure 5.7 The break in

Leaving the current

Leaving the current, or *making a break out* as most paddlers call it, is the sensible way to stop on a river. It gets you into an eddy, facing upstream – a good way to be positioned whether you want to carry on downstream or get out of the boat. Breaking out requires forward planning. You have to know an eddy is coming up (or be looking well ahead to spot one) and a conscious decision has to be made really to go for it.

The break out

- Start the kayak moving towards the eddy line while you are still upstream of it.

- Aim to cross the eddy line at about 45 degrees, using a forward sweep on the downstream side.

- As the nose of the boat crosses the eddy line, raise the downstream edge and support yourself on a low brace on the upstream side.

- As the boat spins in the eddy use a forward stroke to check any slippage downstream which might occur.

The faster the current you are leaving, the faster will be the break out manoeuvre. When you have built up some confidence try using a bow rudder instead of a low brace to pull you out of the current. Again, the edging is crucial in this manoeuvre.

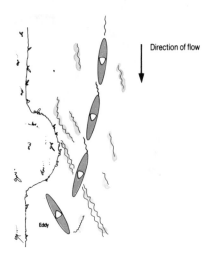

Direction of flow

Eddy

Figure 5.8 The break out

Crossing the current

For this manoeuvre find a wide piece of flow, free from obstructions and eddies. The aim is to begin at the bank, facing upstream, and to cross to the opposite bank without losing ground downstream. It's called a *ferry glide*.

The ferry glide

- Pull into the current either by a draw stroke or paddling forwards.

- Keep the nose of the kayak pointing mainly upstream but slightly towards the far bank.

- Paddle steadily forwards, enough to prevent the boat drifting downstream. It will track across the current.

- If you feel the kayak turning in the current, use sweep strokes to bring it back onto its angle to the current and then continue paddling forward.

The angle of the kayak to the flow is critical. If in doubt set a fine angle; you can easily widen it if necessary.

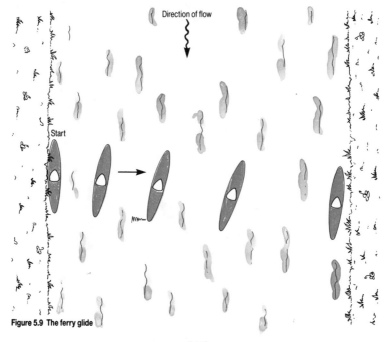

Direction of flow

Start

Figure 5.9 The ferry glide

Once you've got the hang of the ferry glide you'll enjoy the feeling of control it gives you in placing the boat accurately. Your next target is to carry out the same manoeuvre but this time with the boat facing downstream. It's called a *reverse ferry glide*. Paddlers use it when they are suddenly confronted by an obstacle which lies directly downstream of them. If it's too late to break out, you stop by reverse paddling and then reverse ferry glide onto a new line which will take you safely past the obstruction. It's an important technique and one which has saved a few paddlers.

The same principles apply as for the forward ferry glide. Choose a fine angle and control it by using mainly reverse sweep strokes to power you across.

Crossing fast jets of flow

When you want to cross a fast, narrow tongue of water such as you would get with a downstream V, the ferry glide is made at a much faster pace. You drive hard into the current at a shallow angle to the flow and raise the upstream edge as the kayak crosses the eddy line. A few hard strokes on the downstream side and you will blast across the fast tongue of flow into the other eddy. Transfer the edging to the opposite side as you enter the new eddy. This is simply called a *cross*.

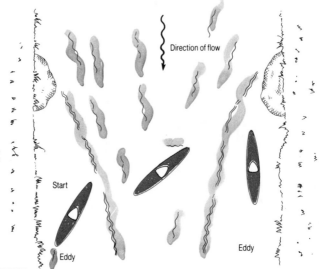

Figure 5.10 The cross

———————————— **Hazards** ————————————

No one needs to be told that white water can be dangerous, but often the apprehension which beginners feel can be dispelled by understanding exactly what is dangerous and what isn't. You need to know specifically what to watch out for. Water which is well beyond your skill or fitness level is the most important hazard to avoid. Having inappropriate boat and equipment is next. You should make certain that these are more than adequate for the degree of paddling you are undertaking.

Now here are some specific features to look out for which can cause problems for paddlers on a river:

Bends

Beginners may be taken by surprise by the power of even a simple current as it accelerates on a bend. Often tree-lined banks have exposed roots and collapsed, overhanging trees touching the water on the outside of bends. On narrow rivers this might block the whole passage. Be aware of this and treat bends with caution. Run through on the inside unless you can see that the outside is completely clear. Go into bends slowly, especially on narrow rivers, and be prepared to use reverse ferry gliding to take you on an accurate, safe line through.

Trees

Trees are a common problem for river paddlers. In swollen conditions a river can rise enough to put branches into the water. You must avoid being carried by the current into these. Stay well clear by keeping to mid-stream. If you do take a swim, keep away from trees.

Weirs

These are man-made steps in the river bed, put there to help regulate the flow. They are very common and some can be run safely by canoeists. Many weirs, however, have powerful recirculating currents which can hold a boat and swimmer. In flood conditions many otherwise safe weirs become killers. There is no simple method of recognising the safe weirs, so you should give them all a wide berth.

◢ Very swollen rivers

In high-flood conditions a river poses a number of dangers to paddlers. All of the above problems tend to come into play and waves and stoppers are often at their most threatening. A high volume flood is much more unforgiving of your mistakes and this *heavy water* as paddlers call it can crush a boat in an instant. You have to think and react extremely fast and you can expect little help from anyone if you get into trouble. Unless you are very competent, the wise thing to do is wait for the flood to subside.

– A training scheme for rough water –

Here is a training scheme to guide you with your plans to improve. The scheme projects over a long period of time – probably years rather than weeks. The five stages are a skeleton plan showing the broad direction of your training. What *you* must do is hang some details on it. This means locating your sites, finding your training partners and organising your equipment. Also, you need to set yourself goals within each of the five stages. Write down your specific goals for the first stage and get to work immediately. Start constructing the specific goals for stage two – you can consolidate and fine tune these when you get started in that stage. Let the forward planning run a natural course. List your goals as you feel right to do so: the longer term ones tend to jump out at you. You can always revise your goals as your training develops.

◢ 1 Flat water stroke work

Perfect all your basic strokes. Rehearse the stroke sequences for breaking out of and into the current. Use floats/markers to force yourself to use accurate boat placement. Try fast turns, slow turns and bow rudders.

◢ 2 Using the simple broad V

Choose a safe site and practise break ins and break outs. Assess each attempt – what went right? Are your success and accuracy improving?

Make full use of this site – invent interesting and challenging manoeuvres for yourself involving crossing as well as turns. Vary everything – speed, point of entry/exit across the eddy line, amount of edging, angle of entry/exit and amount of rest between efforts, etc. You should have at least three separate sessions on this site before moving on.

✖ 3 Change to a different site

As always, think about the safety of the area. Use smaller eddies – behind boulders, bridge piers, etc. Look for eddies where the eddy line is not well defined and learn to break out and in by *feeling* the boat interact with the current differentials. Work in differing water conditions and learn to seek out new eddies. Take time out to watch other paddlers working the river, paying particular attention to those who are very effective but appear to put in little effort. You will need weeks of these sessions.

Your strength and fitness will increase along with your skill and you cannot fail to improve as long as you put in the practice. Get a book on *stretching* and learn how to use this to improve the flexibility of your joints and muscles.

✖ 4 Simple river trips on easy water

Start doing sections of the river which involve a number of rapids and features. Enjoy the scenery and wildlife but also play around on every rapid and eddy. Allow yourself rest periods, but otherwise keep the boat moving continuously down, up and across the flow. Check out every V and eddy – set yourself slalom courses using boulders, bridge arches and gravel banks. Your friends will join in and you'll be amazed at what a little friendly rivalry can do to improve your performance. The more experience you can get on different river sections, the better.

✖ 5 Adventuring on white water

This is where you start challenging yourself on new ground. Running unfamiliar rivers which challenge your skills is about a lot more than just good boat control. It's about preparing equipment, inspecting rapids, reading guide books, looking after your friends and coping with emergencies and lesser problems as they arise on the river. The experience is intense, the commitment is demanding – and the rewards? There's no way I'm going to spoil it for you by describing them here!

Setting goals

When you set yourself goals, choose things which involve a definite outcome, so you can measure your progress against something concrete. Here is an example of a goal structure:

Long-term goal
To successfully and safely run a Grade III river in Scotland.

Medium-term goals
1 To get to three different white water sites and be able to carry out all manoeuvres on them.
2 To run a Grade III river in Wales.
3 To roll successfully after an accidental capsize in white water.

Short-term goals
Can you work out a set of example goals for yourself? Remember that you must be able to see, measure or test the results.

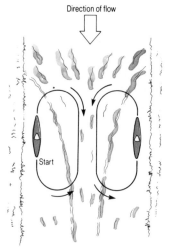

Direction of flow

Start

The basic circuit involves breaking in, descending, and breaking out. Remember to practise left and right. What can you vary in these circuits? Now do it.

Figure 5.11.1 Training on a simple broad V (a)

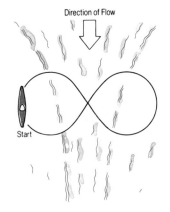

The S-turn. Break in and work your way across as you drift downstream. Follow with a break out. Performed continuously these represent good fitness work and skill training. Keep going until you drop!

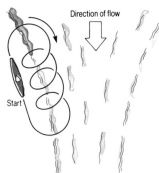

Eddy line spin. Lay the kayak across the eddy line – it spins. Help by using long sweeps.
Variations – remain in one spot or let the boat descend with the flow. Don't forget to use the other eddy line as well.

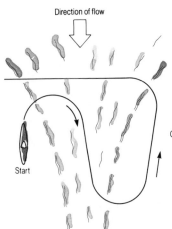

Combine moves. S-turn followed by cross.....and more and more!

Figure 5.11.2 Training on a simple broad V(b)

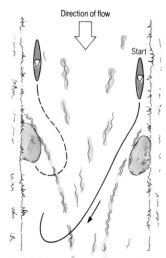

Direction of flow

Start

Remember to work on different approaches. Have you tried paddling back upstream to your starting position yet?

Okay, so now you're confident you can do any manoeuvre – place your boat anywhere you wish in the V.
Now do everything in reverse. Careful, reverse break ins need practice

Figure 5.11.3 Training on a simple broad V(c)

 ——— **Running white water in the ——— open canoe**

Specialist white water open canoes do exist. They are more manoeuvrable and slightly shorter than the conventional touring boat and, importantly, are fitted with a seating arrangement which allows your thighs to be used to control edging, in very much the same way as they do in a kayak. In any type of open canoe, as much additional floating as possible should be introduced to the boat before getting into rough water. Keeping the water out is a priority because it soon swamps the boat and renders it unmanageable. Crash hats, buoyancy aids, etc. are of course essential.

Running white water in the open canoe requires the same basic techniques of the break out and break in, ferry gliding and crossing. One thing you will discover about the canoe is that you have a much better view of the water ahead compared with a kayak paddler. This is a distinct advantage in white water because you can make more informed decisions about route choice and also learn about obstacles sooner.

On the down side of open canoe paddling, however, there is a marked absence of the acceleration which a kayaker has at his/her disposal. Rapids are run in the open canoe with a much more cautious strategy, because of this lack of acceleration. The boat is aligned for the main route, using reverse ferry glides, the final detailed positioning being done with draw strokes and/or pry strokes. Braces are used to steady the boat as it passes through small stoppers or powerful standing waves. In rapids involving tight manoeuvring, through boulder fields for example, the paddler uses reversing strokes to allow the canoe to descend at slower than the current's speed. This makes reverse ferry gliding very easy and, indeed, extremely precise boat positioning in the rapid is possible using this method. Kayak paddlers working in technically difficult water use the same approach.

General safety on white water

'Water isn't dangerous – it's how people behave in it which is the problem.' It's a trite old saying but it couldn't be more true when speaking about white water safety. What is needed is an *attitude* to the river based on respect for what can happen if things go wrong. Being safe on white water demands a *constant* effort on your part. You must develop your white water skills (including eskimo rolling), improve your river judgement, have the right equipment and, most importantly of all, be aware of your own paddling limitations. This *whole* approach to paddling is the only route to safety. If you get lazy or complacent, the river will always be there, waiting to catch you out.

Throw bag

As well as developing your complete self-reliance as a paddler you should also think seriously about how to help other paddlers who might get into trouble. One of the most useful pieces of safety/rescue equipment you can carry on the river is a *throw line*. It is an invaluable tool which has the main function of helping retrieve swimmers, but it has many other uses (appropriate to both kayakers and open canoeists). The best form of throw line is the *throw bag*. Here the rope is stored in a brightly coloured, lightweight bag. In a swimmer rescue, the bag is thrown with the rescuer retaining the free end. The beauty of the throw bag is that it holds the rope safely together until it is needed and forms a good projectile for a throwing rescue. Features of a good throw bag are as follows.

- Made of floating rope of no less than 8 millimetres thickness.
- The rope should be soft and braided, which will be easy to hold under tension.
- It should be between 12 and 15 metres long.
- Both rope and bag should be conspicuously coloured.

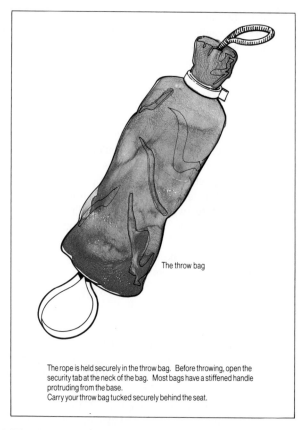

The throw bag

The rope is held securely in the throw bag. Before throwing, open the security tab at the neck of the bag. Most bags have a stiffened handle protruding from the base.
Carry your throw bag tucked securely behind the seat.

Figure 5.12.1 Using a throw bag to help a swimmer (I)

Open the bag at the neck and pull out an arm's length of rope.
Signal/shout to the swimmer.

Take careful aim and then throw. Aim to lay the rope across the swimmer – underarm throwing gives you a good low trajectory. Throw overarm for distances over 12 metres.

Figure 5.12.2 Using a throw bag (II)

There may be a considerable load on the rope when the swimmer takes it up. Always sit and brace yourself after the throw. The swimmer should pull the rope to his/her chest and spread his/her legs.

Figure 5.12.3 Using a throw bag (III)

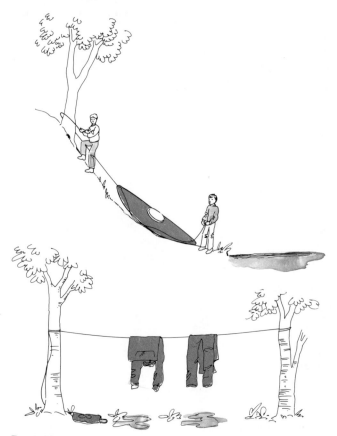

Figure 5.13 Two other uses for the throw bag

✖ *Spare clothing*

A spare sweater and a woolly ski hat carried in a waterproof bag can make a big difference if you or your friends get cold on a trip. It isn't a lot of extra weight and in a watertight bag will provide buoyancy. In the same bag you might like to carry a small first aid kit as well. Think carefully about the jobs you are likely to tackle with the kit before packing it. The main ingredients would be:

- A wound dressing
- Adhesive dressing strip (for blisters)
- Elasticated bandage (for strains and sprains)
- Adhesive tape (for various uses)
- A small pair of scissors
- Safety pins

✖ *EAR*

EAR stands for Expired Air Resuscitation. Every canoeist should consider it a duty to know how to give mouth-to-mouth resuscitation to a non-breathing person. Probably everyone has been taught at some point but you need to refresh your memory. The Appendix at the back of this book shows the exact sequence of actions, but getting properly supervised practice, using a training mannikin, is the only really effective way of doing this.

6

ADVENTURING ON FLAT WATER

A lot of people get a great deal of pleasure from the simple activity of walking – maybe in the hills, on coastal paths or even just in local parks. However short the distance covered, walking brings a unique satisfaction that you have travelled under your own steam at a pace and rhythm which is somehow soothing and therapeutic to mind and body. Flat water paddling can provide this same precious experience.

The sleek hull of the touring boat offers little resistance to the water and only gentle strokes are needed to maintain a steady glide. As with walking, you soon build up your capacity for miles if you do it regularly. This inevitably leads to the delights of planning and dreaming about greater, more extended trips in other parts, maybe even abroad.

Flat water paddling lends itself well to both solo experiences and to getting out with friends. The open canoe and the double kayak make it possible for the very young and the very old to join in. This kind of canoeing really is for everyone. Lots of blind and physically handicapped people participate in flat water canoeing and some even find that their adaptation to disability gives them advantages over able-bodied paddlers.

There are many hundreds of miles of gently flowing or still waters in inland Britain (close on 4000 miles). The vast majority of this can be used by canoeists and is indeed ideal for both simple pottering and extended touring.

———— 'Jogging on water' ————

Paddling is an outstanding form of physical exercise. There are a number of reasons for my saying this. Firstly, exercise physiologists have shown that sustained, vigorous kayak paddling demands massive energy expenditure, comparable to cycling. The raised heart rate and aerobic exercise that come with steady, continuous paddling are exactly right for developing good all-round conditioning. Secondly, paddling is free from the impact loading on joints and muscles which causes so much injury among runners. Thirdly, paddling uses mainly the upper body musculature, strengthening the abdomen and the whole of the back. More conventional exercise, such as running, neglects the arms and trunk completely.

Flat water paddling has been described as 'jogging on water' and that is a very good way of looking at it. You can go at it as easy or as hard as you like. You can extend your mileage with progressively longer trips and, if you so wish, you can set challenges and targets to work towards which involve either paddling with others or working alone.

—— Flat water canoes and kayaks ——

 ## *Kayaks*

You can use any boat on flat water, of course, but since you won't be running white water you might as well choose one which has been designed more with forward speed in mind than manoeuvrability. You might feel that going fast is not important to you but remember that a boat with a fast, directional hull shape will cover any distance with less effort. There will, however, have to be a compromise – very fast kayaks, built for racing, are rather unstable and would not be entirely comfortable for sitting around in on a leisurely tour. The fast tourer possesses the same long, thin lines of the racing kayak but has a hull profile which makes it much more stable to sit in. It might take a few days to get used to the feel of one of these boats but you'll very quickly relate to the business-like way it creams through the water.

A flat water kayak can be built lighter than one made for white water since it doesn't have to take the same amount of 'hammer'. It's worth thinking about getting a 'hand-built' boat (fibre glass or similar) because it is so much lighter than polyethylene. On the other hand if you think it is likely to get some rough treatment (and it might do if you aren't going to be the only user) then a polyethylene touring boat is the right choice.

Your touring kayak will have a large open cockpit with a fixed or removable seat. Internal flotation (fore and aft) is necessary, as are a footrest and a spray cover which allows your knees to bob around in the cockpit. Not all of these boats are fitted with end grab handles and if you never plan to be in water deeper than you can stand up in, then it's probably OK. My advice is to try to have them.

Rudders are popular on flat water kayaks. They allow you to keep all your energy concentrated on moving forwards. Because the steering is controlled by your feet working a tiller bar those correcting strokes are totally unnecessary. Rudders really do make a difference, and all racing kayaks are fitted with them. What you lose with a rudder is some of the kayak's versatility of movement. Reversing isn't so easy (unless your rudder is retractable) and also the whole mechanism needs a little looking after. You really have to decide how much serious touring you intend to do before you can make your mind up about a rudder.

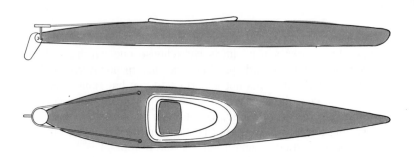

The fast touring single – length just over 500 cm – width approx. 52 cm. The seat is adjustable. A rudder is fitted – the control being a tiller bar which projects from the footrest. This boat would be adequate to compete in lower divisions of marathon racing. Construction – fibreglass or similar hand-built material.

Figure 6.1 Flat water kayaks

A more general purpose flat water tourer.

Length 440 cm – width around 60 cm. Once again the long, open cockpit and long waterline characterise this boat. Construction – polyethylene or fibreglass.

Figure 6.2   Flat water kayaks (cont.)

✔ *Open canoes*

Open canoes are literally made for flat water touring. Leaving aside their rather limited top cruising speed, it's hard to imagine any boat better suited for steady tripping. Some huge unsupported journeys have been achieved in the USA, Canada and Africa using open canoes. The carrying capacity for equipment and food is impressive and as good as any mule! The canoe can be paddled in various positions, and may be guided through shallow water by poling from a standing position. All this and you still have the option of travelling solo or double – it really is a magnificent machine.

More specialised marathon open canoes have narrower, sharper hulls. They are made in double *and* single form and are, of course, extremely light. For short cruises or high-speed touring with road transport support, these canoes just might have their uses for even the non-competing paddler. One very noticeable thing about these boats is that they are paddled not with J strokes but by switching sides every ten strokes or so. The paddles are very short, with a shallow bend in the shaft and these are used at a very high stroke rate.

—— Clothing and equipment for —— flat water

▨ *Paddles*

The flat water kayaker, like the open canoeist, can get away with using just about any kind of paddle, but because there are no great loads being exerted upon it you might think about going for something light-weight. Also, since flat water paddling is mainly about moving forward efficiently, and fancy turning strokes just aren't relevant, you could go for blades built especially for the job. The purpose-made paddle I am describing is referred to as *asymmetric* and is similar to those used by marathon or sprint racers. The blades are *spooned* so that they grip the water more effectively and are shaped in a way which gives a superbly balanced entry and pull in the water. These paddles are an absolute delight to use but, as is always the case with lightweight equipment, you have to treat them with tender loving care.

Figure 6.3 Asymetric kayak paddles

☒ *Buoyancy aids*

Once again, lightness is something you can take advantage of. I recommend one of the pull-over-the-head type buoyancy aids made with lightweight flotation foam. These are compact and yet still efficient if you take a swim. They come in radical colours too!

Figure 6.4 Lightweight buoyancy aid

▨ *Kayak spray deck*

For the kayak paddler, a spray deck is worth having even if you intend never to get so much as the deck wet. On cold days or in wet weather, you'll be glad of it. A spray deck will also let you tackle low grade white water, albeit on a very simple basis.

Figure 6.5 Nylon spray deck

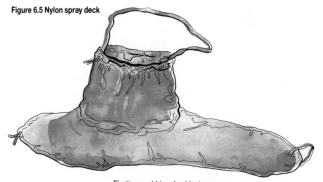

Elastic or webbing shoulder tape sewn
to the tube is a big help on cold, wet days.

◪ *Clothing*

On a warm summer's day you can enjoy your paddling in just shorts and a T-shirt. It's a good habit to have your canoe cag in the back in case the wind gets up. In colder weather a more studied approach to clothing is needed. Remember that paddling is hot work – while you're cruising along you will be warm, possibly even hot, almost regardless of the weather. If you stop for any reason, to portage around a lock or take a picture say, your heat production will plummet and the cold will soon get through.

The answer is to develop a hillwalking psychology and carry a simple bag with spare clothing, etc. with you. One small or medium-sized waterproof bag can carry clothing, food, a small first aid kid, a camera, money, etc. for a day trip. It will go in the rear of the boat, alongside the buoyancy block, and you'll not know it's there.

A basic clothing system for paddling would be a long-sleeved thermal vest, nylon track pants, socks and training shoes. In colder weather a pair of thermal tights under the track pants is a good idea since legs, especially knees, can get a bit chilled. Any non-cotton garment will do over the vest and a fleece or pile sweater (synthetic fabric) is the ideal reserve to have in the bag. If you haven't already got a ski hat then you'll need to find something. Get one which has plenty of knitted tension so that it grips the head tightly, even when soaked through with rain water. Traditional-minded open canoeists should get their hands on a (simulated) racoon skin Davey Crocket style hat if they want to look right at the local trading post!

Select a canoe cag which has an opening neckpiece. This allows you to ventilate and also makes the jacket easier to get off and on. A tuck-away hood is very useful, as is a front pocket. Lightweight waterproof trousers are important if you are planning to walk around in cold weather. There is huge heat loss from the thighs and groin area and so the windproofing performance of these trousers is important for heat conservation. If you can afford it get trousers which are made from breathable fabric, i.e. which allow moisture (vapour) to escape but prevent water from coming in. These are good because they drastically reduce condensation and also allow clothes underneath to dry out while you are walking around. Try to get a pair with tapered legs as they are less likely to catch on things in the boat.

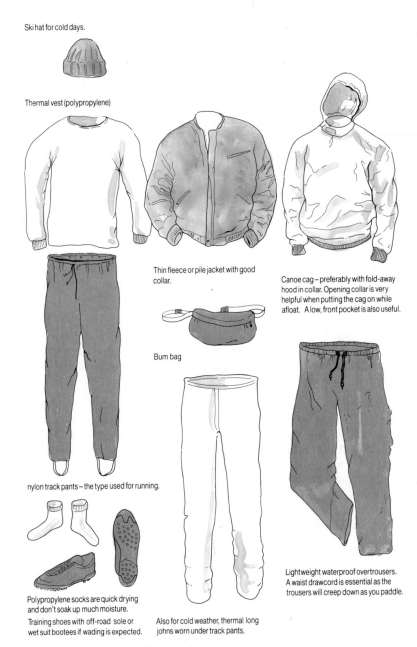

Ski hat for cold days.

Thermal vest (polypropylene)

Thin fleece or pile jacket with good collar.

Bum bag

Canoe cag – preferably with fold-away hood in collar. Opening collar is very helpful when putting the cag on while afloat. A low, front pocket is also useful.

nylon track pants – the type used for running.

Polypropylene socks are quick drying and don't soak up much moisture.

Training shoes with off-road sole or wet suit bootees if wading is expected.

Also for cold weather, thermal long johns worn under track pants.

Lightweight waterproof overtrousers. A waist drawcord is essential as the trousers will creep down as you paddle.

Figure 6.6 Clothing for flat water paddling

⊠ *Carrying gear*

Canoe shops carry waterproof bags which are a size to fit any kayak. They are sausage-shaped and made from PVC or proofed nylon with a closure which ensures complete waterproofing. You can always make your own bags by purchasing neoprene-proofed nylon. Use good quality adhesive and you won't believe how easy these are to make.

Making a waterproof bag

- Cut out a square about 50 × 50 centimetres.
- Draw a 2 centimetre border around the edges of three sides of the neoprene side of the fabric.
- Apply an even coating of waterproof, impact adhesive to the border (on the neoprene side).
- When the adhesive is tacky, fold the fabric to a rectangle so that the edges bond. You can reinforce the seams by cutting 3 centimetre strips of fabric and glueing these around the outer edges.

This gives a remarkably good and inexpensive bag. You can cut bags to suit your own requirements – to fit a tent or sleeping bag, etc. The bag is sealed with the simplest and most inexpensive of items – a rubber band cut from a car inner tube. Once you get into the way of making your own equipment (and using the right adhesive is really the secret) all sorts of things are possible.

The size of the bag is much less critical in the open canoe. A mountaineering rucksack with the equipment packed into a waterproof polythene liner will do well. Some paddlers even use rigid polythene storage drums with self-sealing lids. These are rather heavy but are bombproof for wear and tear. For carrying things like a hat, paddle mitts, a penknife and sunglasses you will find a simple *bumbag* very useful. You can paddle quite happily with this around your waist and when you need to get something just spin it around to the front. Bumbags are inexpensive and you really don't need a fancy one.

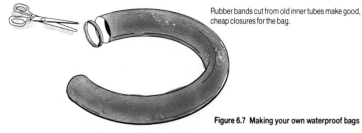

Rubber bands cut from old inner tubes make good, cheap closures for the bag.

Figure 6.7 Making your own waterproof bags

Four steps to making a bag

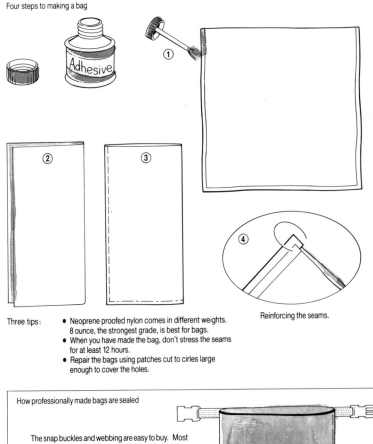

Reinforcing the seams.

Three tips:
- Neoprene proofed nylon comes in different weights. 8 ounce, the strongest grade, is best for bags.
- When you have made the bag, don't stress the seams for at least 12 hours.
- Repair the bags using patches cut to cirles large enough to cover the holes.

How professionally made bags are sealed

The snap buckles and webbing are easy to buy. Most sewing machines could handle this job, or it could be done by hand. Stitching is rendered waterproof by smearing the inside threads and holes with adhesive.

The mouth of the bag is stretched tight and then rolled downwards a few times. This makes it bombproof!

Figure 6.7 (cont.)

◩ *Carrying a map or guide*

To be totally self-contained on unfamiliar waters you need to carry a map. Keeping track of your mileage and checking out the features of the surrounding countryside is all part of the enjoyment of the journey. Maps, however, are rarely water resistant and to keep one in reasonable condition on even a day trip takes a bit of thought. There are a number of effective possibilities.

● Fold the map working side uppermost and seal it into a strong polythene bag. Use fabric tape to seal it – you should be able to open and reseal as often as necessary. Purpose-built map cases are easily available through outdoor shops. These are inexpensive and worth considering.

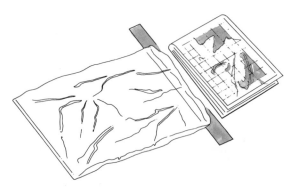

A strong polyethylene bag sealed with fabric tape gives a waterproof and versatile holder. Expel the air before sealing, and once sealed the package can be folded to fit your pocket or bumbag.

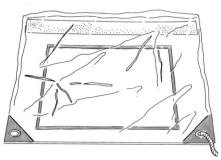

Hillwalker's map case with holes for carrying string. The seal is made with velcro – 'not 100% watertight – and designed to work best when hung by the string.

Figure 6.8 Carrying your map

- Before leaving on your trip stick the map onto the foredeck using adhesive transparent film. This will mean cutting out the section of the required map first.
- Use transparent adhesive film to seal both sides of the section of map you need. A laminating machine will do the same job neatly.

Personally, I prefer not to have my map stuck to the deck. This means I can take it with me when roaming around on land. However, if you are likely to have to map-read while keeping both hands on the paddle (as sea kayakers do) then on the deck, directly in front of the cockpit, is the place to have it. You can have the best of both worlds by drilling the deck and inserting two shock-cord bands crossways on the foredeck. These will hold the map firmly in place and yet allow you to remove it easily.

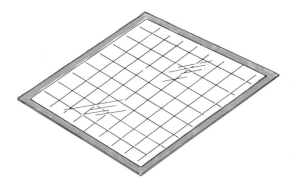

The main section cut from a map and laminated either with transparent film or heat sealer. Remember that this system allows for both sides to be used.

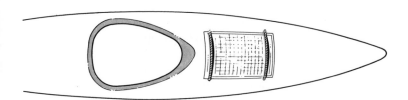

Shock cord (elastic rope) can be threaded into the deck to give a really secure map holder and the holes can be sealed using silicone sealant. The cords can also hold a torch while you navigate a tunnel, for example.

Figure 6.8 (cont.)

Camping

The average canoe or kayak can carry a lot more gear than the average rucksack, so camping is definitely a possibility. Before you get too carried away with tents, have a think to see if you can cope with a simpler form of shelter. Bivvi bags are great for one night trips and for much longer in good weather. A breathable bag would cost (and weigh) a lot less than a tent. Of course you could travel really cheaply and use a polythene survival bag.

A stove and sleeping bag are the only other specialist requirements. Money spent on these items is never wasted. Gas stoves are clean and simple but can be difficult in a wind. Pressure stoves which use petrol or kerosene tend to be reliable workhorses.

Always pack your boat in a way that takes account of its trim. Aim to have it set level – if this isn't possible, stern down is usually preferable to bow down. In a kayak, keep the cockpit area completely free of equipment of any kind. An open canoe is a dream to run a camping trip from. You can take plenty of luxuries and packing is easy. On land the canoe can provide one side of your improvised shelter.

 ## Competing on flat water

However uncompetitive you might feel you may well find great satisfaction in marathon racing. As with road running, a canoe marathon is very much about challenging *yourself* as much as others. Doing this in the presence of other racers adds to the atmosphere and helps to motivate you to improve. Unlike road racing, canoeing does not set a rigid distance for all marathons. There is a ranking or divisional system in most countries and the lower divisions often race shorter distances. Most marathons are between 16 and 32 kilometres in length but there are some much longer events around the world. The most famous of these is the Devizes to Westminster – a distance of 125 miles with some 70 odd *portages* (leaving the water to carry your boat) around canal locks. An average time for this race is around 21 hours.

Most races, however, have a time of under two hours. You will need a fast touring boat or a pure racing machine in order to compete seriously. Racing paddlers put many hours into their training and the calendar is packed with events. There are classes for men, ladies, juniors and veterans. The boat classes are kayak singles (K1) as well as doubles (K2) and canoes. Many clubs are entirely dedicated to racing and are very willing to help beginners get involved. This is probably the best way to get into this aspect of canoeing as you can get all of the information you need about races, divisions, equipment, etc from the club. However, if you aren't a club type of person it is still perfectly possible to compete by getting your own equipment together and referring to the events calendar produced by the national governing body. Some canoeing magazines also produce calendars of events.

 —————— **Access to UK water** ——————

In the UK not all waterways carry the right to public navigation. A landowner who owns both river banks may require you to get permission before passing through, and of course the same applies to crossing land in order to get to a river. The British Canoe Union operates a local river advisory scheme which can provide paddlers with access information on rivers where this is necessary. (See p. 167 for details.)

The superb canal network which covers most of Britain is controlled by British Waterways. A licence is required for any boat using the canal system and the British Canoe Union membership includes one of these. British Waterways encourage the use of their canals for recreation and provide an excellent range of publications (maps, leaflets, etc.) which would be useful to the paddler. The address for British Waterways is on p. 170.

 —————————— **Europe** ——————————

The touring paddler has a lot to go at in Europe. France, especially, has many fine rivers which offer enormous potential, with some 8000 km of navigable waterways. The French Canoe Federation (FFCK) publish an excellent general map showing the canoeable water, canals, etc. and this also contains useful information on obtaining more specific details about individual regions. (The FFCK address is on p. 168.)

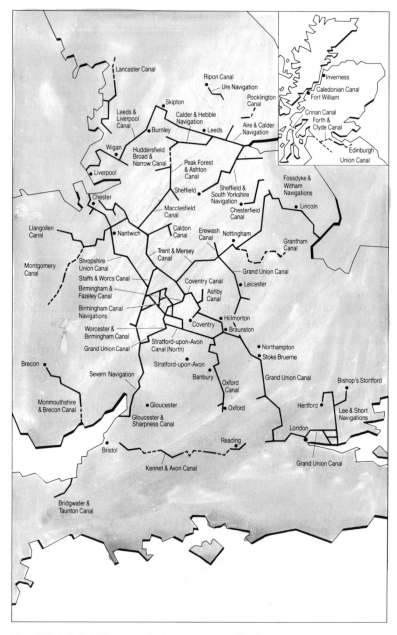

Figure 6.9 Touring in the UK. The canals and main waterway systems of Britain.

An important UK contact for anyone to make when planning a trip in Europe is the International Long River Canoeist Club. Their address is on p. 170.

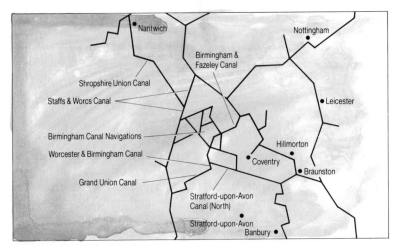

Figure 6.10 Canals of the West Midlands

 ———————— **USA and Canada** ————————

The magnificent lakes and extensive river systems of Canada and the USA are a flat water tourer's paradise. The potential for long journeys, often in wilderness country, is virtually boundless. There are many canoe trails and a wide range of guide books are available to help with planning and route finding. American canoeists have produced some excellent technical books on using the open canoe for wilderness journeys. One such book is highly recommended – *The Path of The Paddle* by Bill Mason.

Both the USA and Canada have plenty of canoeing outfitters. These shops often operate a canoe hire service and finding a rental agent near popular paddling locations is rarely a problem.

Remember, of course, that it is quite feasible to fly with a kayak. If it is long, smaller aircraft may not be able to take it in the hold. It's worth making tentative enquiries by phone first and then arriving at the check-in with the boat as baggage.

7

—— SEA TOURING ——

Almost all canoeing which takes place on the sea is done in kayaks, so this section will deal with kayaking only. The open canoe *can* be used in expert hands on the open sea, but its high above-water profile can cause serious problems in a wind. Sea kayaking, like white water paddling, slalom racing, etc. is a sport in its own right and any paddler has a great deal to learn before considering himself an expert in this area. The sea, however close we may feel to it along our coastline, is a serious place upon which to adventure in a man-powered craft. Sea kayaking demands more knowledge and experience to do it safely than any other form of paddling. *Please do not consider going alone on the sea in your kayak until you have several years of sea paddling behind you.*

The sea kayaker is very much like the mountaineer. Journeys are made in wild country where help is not readily to hand. Retreating to safety if things go even slightly wrong is often difficult and understanding your own limitations is paramount. Safety is based, first and foremost, on well-informed planning and thorough preparation of equipment. Being able to take care of yourself is also essential, as is the knowledge and training to be able to give support or assistance to another paddler.

—————— Getting started ——————

The most important thing to do is get one, or preferably two, other paddlers to go along with. If they are experienced sea paddlers you will learn quickly from them by watching how they plan trips, make decisions and handle their boats.

You can start sea journeying using a basic closed cockpit kayak provided it has all of the following:

- Internal flotation in good condition, plus additional air bags to give maximum flotation.
- End grabs in good condition. Decklines are even better.
- Sound sea worthiness. There must be no leaks in deck or hull and the construction must be strong.
- Medium to high volume. Kayaks which are built to sit low on the water or even below it (slalom) are not suitable for sea touring.
- A strong footrest which will not trap your feet if they pass forward of it.

In addition, a good watertight spray deck is essential, as well as a sound paddle and properly fitting buoyancy aid. A wetsuit is strongly advisable for your sea trips, because the sea is always cold, even in the warmest of weather.

When and where to start

Your early sea-going experiences should all be made in fine weather, i.e. calm or light winds, and in good sea conditions with no breaking waves or swell. Use a stretch of coastline where easy landings can be made at any point – gravel or sandy beaches are ideal. Keep close to the shore and travel along just getting used to the feel of your kayak on the ocean. You cannot fail to sense the vastness of the sea and even on the calmest of days you will feel something of the colossal energy stored in its movements. If this makes you feel humbled then it's a good thing because the paddler who has respect for the sea will go far and last long.

A conventional white water type kayak will have to be kept on a tight rein on the sea, especially if there is a wind and a 'ruffle' of small waves. You will be constantly correcting and steering as you travel. If you aren't attempting large passages this is no big problem, but it is tiring work for a beginner and you should set yourself only short distances of a mile or so to cover in the first few trips. Building up endurance is a crucial part of becoming a sea canoeist – you need lots of 'miles in your arms' to help you journey further and also to give you a good reserve in case things go wrong.

Basic equipment for a sea trip

- Spare paddles – carry inside or, better, outside the kayak
- Waterproof equipment bag(s)
- Polythene survival bag
- Spare sweater
- Overtrousers
- Lunch and a hot drink
- First aid kit
- Warm hat
- Penknife (stainless)
- Basic compass
- Sun cream/sunglasses
- Bumbag
- Flares – could be carried in pockets in a buoyancy aid or in bumbag
- A map or chart can be fixed to the deck
- A simple repair kit (a role of fabric 'canoe tape' or plumbers' instant repair tape – this remains gooey and will stick to anything so cut it into strips and lay it between two sheets of polythene)

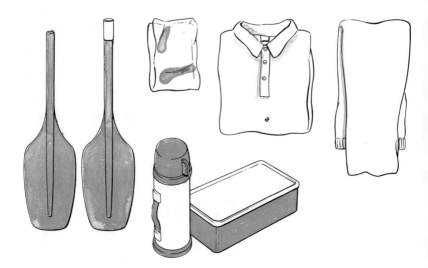

Figure 7.7.1 Basic equipment for a sea trip (I)

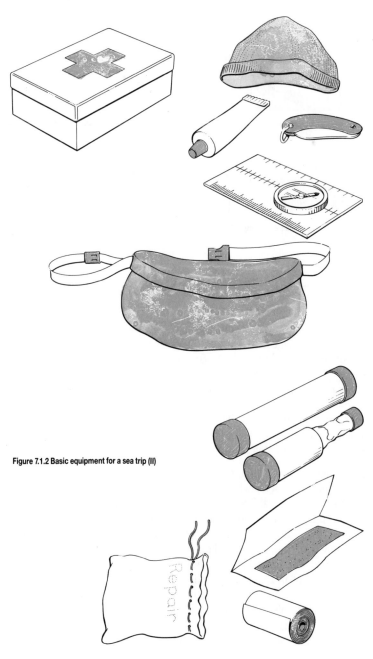

Figure 7.1.2 Basic equipment for a sea trip (II)

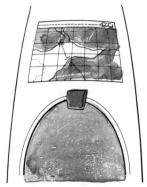
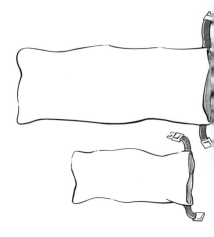

Figure 7.1.3 Basic equipment for a sea trip (III)

──────── The sea kayak ────────

The modern sea-touring kayak is a highly specialised machine. Forward speed, low windage and equipment carrying capacity figure highly in the design criteria. Most kayaks are handbuilt in glass fibre or a similar material, while a few are rotomoulded in polyethylene. Cockpits are small so that water is excluded and most kayaks have watertight bulkheads fore and aft. These are sealed compartments with hatch access through the decks. The compartments carry equipment (food, camping gear, etc.) for your trip. Magnificent wilderness journeys are possible because of this stowage space.

A good paddler can average 3 knots in reasonable conditions and can make progress in seas which would cause major difficulties for other small boats. Sea kayaks are commonly fitted with a bilge pump. This makes it possible to empty the heavy kayak without the hassle of turning it over and raising the ends. The pump handle is on deck, within reach of the cockpit. The large rear deck area of the kayak makes it possible to carry some equipment there. Typically the spare paddles are kept in this space, under shock cord loops. In front of the cockpit the kayak has more deck fittings to allow charts, cag, etc. to be carried. Here also is the position for the compass, which is usually removable. On large crossings, at night and in poor visibility the compass is an essential piece of equipment: learn to use it.

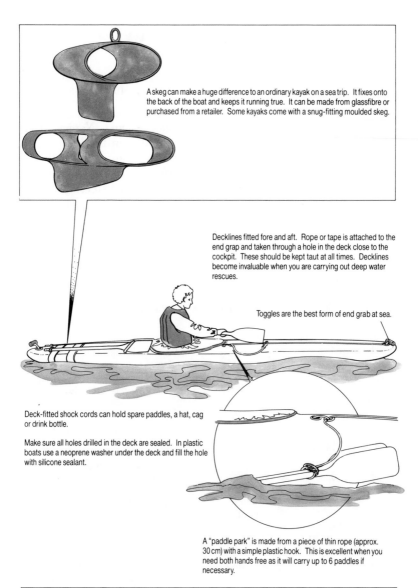

A skeg can make a huge difference to an ordinary kayak on a sea trip. It fixes onto the back of the boat and keeps it running true. It can be made from glassfibre or purchased from a retailer. Some kayaks come with a snug-fitting moulded skeg.

Decklines fitted fore and aft. Rope or tape is attached to the end grap and taken through a hole in the deck close to the cockpit. These should be kept taut at all times. Decklines become invaluable when you are carrying out deep water rescues.

Toggles are the best form of end grab at sea.

Deck-fitted shock cords can hold spare paddles, a hat, cag or drink bottle.

Make sure all holes drilled in the deck are sealed. In plastic boats use a neoprene washer under the deck and fill the hole with silicone sealant.

A "paddle park" is made from a piece of thin rope (approx. 30 cm) with a simple plastic hook. This is excellent when you need both hands free as it will carry up to 6 paddles if necessary.

Some older designs of kayak (fibreglass/general purpose) are ideal for sea touring. They are usually around 400 cm long and have a strong watertight deck and hull which is essential. Old foam flotation can be replaced with new blocks of polyethylene glued or held in place with resin.

Figure 7.2 A closed cockpit adapted for sea touring

The weather and you

Basically, weather is composed of the following entities as far as the sea paddler is concerned: wind, visibility, precipitation and air temperature.

Of these, one holds overriding significance – *wind*. Nothing, and I mean nothing, causes problems for the paddler in the way that the wind can. Without wind the sea would remain calm except in the few areas where strong tides exist. A headwind can reduce your forward progress to less than a crawl. A side wind can make steering a misery and even a following wind can cause serious problems as you catapult down one wave after another. A wind can cause the surface of an otherwise peaceful sea to turn into breaking peaks which demand hard, defensive paddling in order to stay upright.

The Beaufort windscale

Force	Speed in Knots	Forecasting Term	Sea Conditions
0	1 or less	calm	like a mirror
1	1–3	light air	ripples like scales
2	4–6	light breeze	small wavelets, not breaking
3	7–10	gentle breeze	large wavelets, crests begin to break
4	11–16	moderate breeze	small waves becoming longer, fairly frequent white horses
5	17–21	fresh breeze	moderate waves with many white horese
6	22–27	strong breeze	large waves begin to form, white crests more extensive everywhere
7	28–33	near gale	sea heaps up with white foam from breaking waves
8	34–40	gale	moderately high waves of greater length, much foam
9	41–47	strong gale	high waves, dense streaks of foam along the direction of the wind
10	48–55	storm	
11	56–65	severe storm	
12	66+	hurricane	

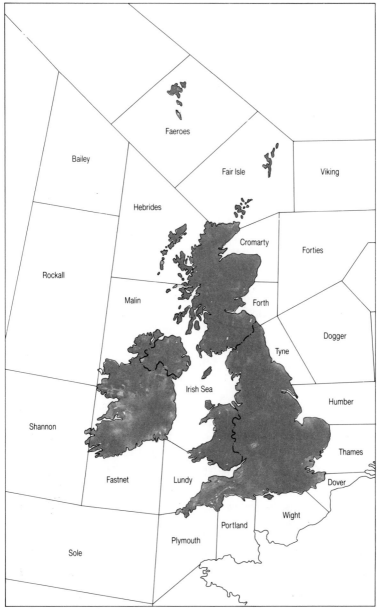

The shipping forecasts are broadcast on BBC Radio 4. An inshore waters (coastal) forecast is also broadcast around 30 minutes past midnight.

Figure 7.3 The shipping forecast sea areas

Forecasters and coastguards refer to the wind strength in terms of the *Beaufort scale*. Sometimes wind speed is given in knots – the chart shows how the Beaufort numbers 1–12 relate to wind speed in knots. Beginners usually start to struggle at wind strength 3 or 4.

The sea paddler has to be a student of the weather. This means developing a thirst for weather forecasts, learning to read weather maps and recognise typical patterns. Modern weather forecasting is very accurate, especially up to 24 hours ahead. You should find out where to get coastal forecasts as well as land based. In the UK the Meteorological Office provides superb forecasts for shipping which are broadcast on Radio 4 four times a day. The whole of the sea around the British Isles is divided into *sea areas* for the purposes of these forecasts but you will need to get some practice at listening to and interpreting them. A telephone service, *Marinecall*, is another extremely useful source of forecasts for the paddler. Remember that you always need to know two things about the wind – its strength and its direction. A wind blowing *offshore* will take you directly out to sea, if you allow yourself to drift and, furthermore, it will blow harder the further out you get. An *onshore* wind takes you towards the shore but is likely to cause breaking waves at your landing site.

The tides and you

Tides are compelling and fascinating to the sea kayaker. How is it that these vast, deep ponds, the earth's oceans, rise and fall? The paddler soon realises that the sea is not only constantly on the move with wave action but also that it is streaming and surging around the coastlines like a huge river. Unlike a river, however, these *tidal streams* reverse direction four times a day.

In practical terms the paddler needs to be aware of the rise and fall of the tide, *tidal range*, simply because a low tide could mean a long carry to or from the water's edge. The British coast has some large tidal ranges (a rise and fall of 3 metres is not uncommon). Times of high and low water can be worked out using local tide tables which include the range.

Although not all parts of the coast are affected by strong tidal streams, the paddler needs to be aware of them wherever he or she goes. Admiralty charts as well as tidal stream atlases contain the information needed on stream direction and rate. The rate or speed of a stream is recorded in knots (nautical miles per hour). A tidal stream of say 4 knots doesn't sound much, but it is very unlikely that you could even hold your ground if you had to paddle against it. Any paddler working in an area where the streams get to this rate is operating in serious sea kayaking conditions. As a beginner you should choose to paddle only in areas where tidal streams are negligible or non-existent. There are plenty of these around.

The flood stream is in operation while the tide is rising from low to high water. This lasts for approximately 6.25 hours. At high water there is a short period of slack and then the ebb stream starts up, again for approximately 6.25 hours, until low water and another short period of slack is reached. This accounts for the occurence of two high and two low waters in each 25 hour period.

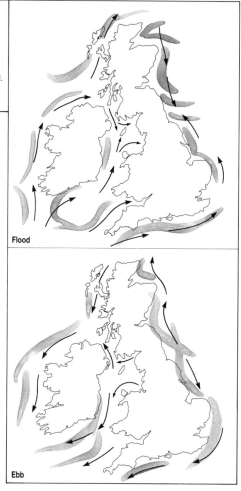

Flood

Ebb

Figure 7.4   General direction of flow of tidal streams around the British Isles

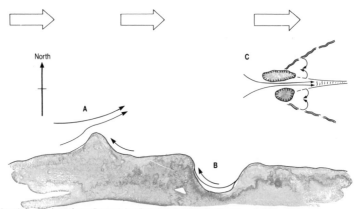

If you look at a piece of coastline more locally you can see that the streams are in fact much more interesting than the general map of Britain shows. Although the main direction of the stream offshore is eastwards the paddler working close to the shore meets a number of variations: Point A is a headland where the stream is deflected and accelerated to the north east; Point B is a bay, here there is an eddy close inshore; Point C between the islands the stream is squeezed and accelerated. Eddies occur downstream of the islands. The paddler could expect rough water at A and C. The tidal streams behave very much like an enormous river, but remember the direction (and rate) of flow changes periodically.

Figure 7.5 The stream close to shore

Paddling skills

As a sea paddler you must have mastered the basic strokes of kayaking (see pp. 56–94) before even thinking about a sea trip. For holding a course in a choppy sea, and making a landing through waves you must be especially expert with the stern rudder. Also the high and low brace are essential if you are to remain upright in anything other than flat calm conditions.

Eskimo rolling

My advice is to treat learning to roll as a priority. The sea has a way of catching you out when you least expect it and if you can roll you can avert a potential crisis in an instant. The difference between rolling upright to carry on and capsizing to become a helpless swimmer is obviously enormous. Remember that being self-reliant is the aim (and duty) of every sea paddler.

Learning to roll in a swimming pool is only half way to being competent. Instinctive rolling in cold water demands training, effort and a lot of practice.

Surfing

Riding waves in a kayak is fantastic fun – in fact it is a sport in its own right. The sea paddler needs surfing skills to negotiate landings and launching in rough conditions. The brace, stern rudder and eskimo roll are the basic tools which the surfer uses to play with the kayak in waves.

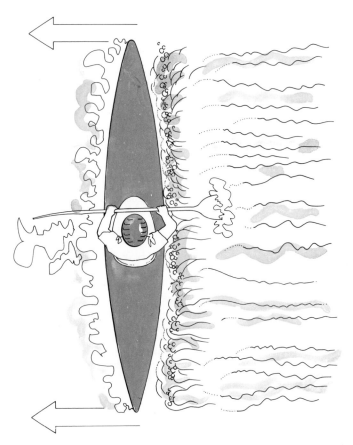

Once a wave breaks while you are surfing you have no choice but to run sideways on it. To stay upright you must brace on the wave – using its energy as a handrail. This is called a "bongo ride" because in big surf the wave bounces the boat uncontrollably.

If a braking wave hits you side-on this is how you should deal with it – even if it isn't a planned surfing session!

Figure 7.6 Surfing – using a brace on a wave

Start off in small surf and get used to side surfing in the shallow water. Here the waves are broken and a brace on top of the wave will keep you upright. With a partner nearby, move a little further out and start to run straight in before the kayak is swung sideways by the break. On unbroken waves use a stern rudder to hold the boat on its ride. Run diagonally with the stern rudder trailing to the *shoreward* side.

Wear a helmet when practising in the surf, and the quicker you learn to roll the sooner will you be able to enjoy real surfing. Once a kayak takes off on a wave it builds up considerable speed. Colliding with another kayak, or worse an innocent swimmer, could have grim consequences. For this reason stay well clear of swimmers and board surfers while you are kayak surfing.

Deep water rescues

Helping a capsized paddler empty and get back into the boat without going ashore is called a *deep water rescue. This is an essential skill for any paddler going onto the sea.*

Deep water rescue

- Paddle towards the swimmer, who should be holding onto the end of his kayak.

- Get the swimmer to hold the end of your boat – you take the end of his boat from him.

- Pull the swamped boat across your cockpit until it tips and spills water – slide it back until water spills again.

- Roll the boat upright on your cockpit and then slide it into the water facing in the opposite direction to your own.

- Bring the swimmer between the boats with his arms hooked over each. He lies back and hooks his own cockpit with his feet. This allows him to raise his bottom and drop it into the cockpit, with you steadying the whole raft. He should pull the two kayaks together under his back as he does this. From here he manoeuvres himself properly into the boat seat.

These rescues are much easier said than done. There are many tricks and tips to learn before you will be able to pull off a quick rescue in even simple conditions. Practice is absolutely essential – for everyone. If *you* become the swimmer, the whole thing is much easier if you know what is going on and have been involved in practice in the past. By all means do your first rehearsals in the swimming pool, but make sure you practise in real (but safe) deep water.

Emptying the swimmer's kayak is the first job. Form a
T with it and then quickly lift its nose onto your cockpit.
Slide it towards you until the cockpit is directly over
yours. Deck lines make this much easier.

The swimmer can help by pulling down to spill the
water. *Never lose contact with the swimmer.*

Getting the swimmer back in is not easy. Both of you
must work to hold the two boats together. Also you
should lean across the other boat to help keep it level
as the paddler climbs back in.

Figure 7.7.1 Deep water rescue (I)

Here's another way of getting him/her back in. Try it and see which you prefer. This time the swimmer pulls on the paddle and cockpit until he is lying on the boat. A bit of wriggling and jiggling is required to get into the seat but it works fine.
Practise deep water rescues-don't let your first attempt be a real rescue.
Figure 7.7.2 Deep water rescue (II)

Rafting at sea

A group of kayaks joined up alongside each other is called a *raft*; the simplest being composed of two boats. Rafts can be useful for keeping a group together when it has stopped paddling, giving support to a paddler who has suddenly become nervous or ill or doing any job which requires a paddler to get out of his boat for a short time (he sits on the raft).

Rafts are held together by paddlers gripping the cockpit rim of the boat(s) next to them. You must be careful not to lose paddles. Rafts are *not* suitable when conditions are rough (in breaking waves) since there is a real danger that the kayaks will ride over the top of each other and squash the contents!

Try using a two man raft to carry out a deep water rescue. This is a much more reliable way to rescue someone in bad conditions – providing you are well practised.

———————— Planning a trip ————————

A sea trip needs to be researched. That's not a problem, in fact it's part of the fun. The kind of things you must find out are: the distance of the journey, the road access, the landing points, the tidal streams and the time of high/low water. On the day you will need a weather forecast and you should always know the kind of conditions which would cancel the trip.

Distance and coastal features can be extracted from either an ordnance survey map or a chart. (On a chart you measure in nautical miles.) If you are working in an area with tidal streams of 1 knot or more a chart would be needed. Naturally you should plan the trip so that you travel *with* the tidal stream. If crossing to an island the period of slack (when the stream changes direction) is a good time to move. Remember that, just like the current in a river, tidal flow forms eddies behind obstructions. The scale of the eddies can vary enormously so, when route finding in tidal streams, it pays to think like a river canoeist, eddy hopping if you have to paddle against the flow and staying in the mainstream when going with it.

Before leaving on a trip think hard about the equipment you will need. Spare clothing, first aid kit and survival bags are the basics and these should be secured well into the kayaks so that they will not be a hindrance in the event of a deep water rescue. A set of split paddles carried as spares is usually carried by a group at sea and is a very wise precaution. You will need food and fluids to drink as well – paddling needs to be fuelled.

Finally, be prepared to cancel or abort your trip at any stage. This is a sensible and safe psychology upon which to base your journeying.

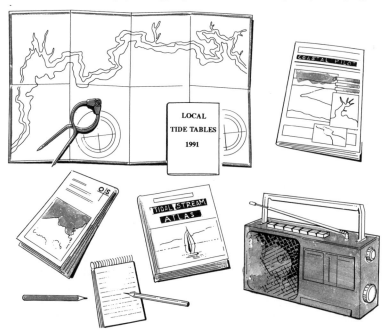

Figure 7.8 Resources for planning a sea trip

- An admiralty chart gives vital information about tides, depths, buoys, etc. The scale on the sides of a chart is latitude. 1 minute of latitude = 1 nautical mile.

- A tidal stream atlas gives general tidal streams in large area and hour by hour diagrams of rate and direction of flow.

- A coastal pilot gives written information about tides and other relevant material.

- Local tide-tables have times of high and low water for every day of the year.

- Dividers are good for measuring distance accurately from the chart or map.

- A pencil and notebook are useful for recording times and other details as you make your plans. A chinagraph pencil will write important details such as tide times on the deck of your kayak.

- Charts give only limited information about land features such as roads. An ordnance survey map can be very helpful for working out campsites, access, stores, etc.

- Don't forget the weather forecast.

Safety at sea

If you do set off on a coastal trip, however short, make sure that you leave notification of your journey with someone responsible. This person can alert the coastguard if you don't turn up within the time specified for the end of your trip. It's a simple but important precaution. In emergencies the coastguard in the UK may be reached through the usual 999 telephone emergency system.

Emergency signalling

If you do get into trouble at sea and can't handle it yourself then you need help. Summoning help is easy if you have a powerful, functioning radio but canoeists are rarely able to carry such equipment. Help is summoned by trying to attract attention and for this flares are the most common method. Carrying flares is definitely no guarantee that you will be rescued but it is still a worthwhile precaution to take. To attract attention, flares which fire projectiles are best, the parachute flare being the most effective. To pinpoint your position for rescuers, smoke (daylight only) or red handflares are equally good. Remember that three kayaks are nothing more than tiny specks on the surface of a huge expanse of water – keep this in mind if you're nervous about handing over money for flares.

When carrying flares, store them where you can reach them without having to get out of the kayak. Talk to other sea paddlers about this and get some ideas. Also, remember that your flares have an expiry date beyond which their performance is in question. Read the instructions on the flare casing and think how you will carry them out in a rough sea.

8

GETTING INFORMATION

Finding out more about the sport

This book is written to help you to get yourself started. There will always be plenty more to find out about canoeing and there are many ways to do this. Mixing with other paddlers is one of the best, and also it makes safety sense. Below are some suggestions for other ways to find answers to your questions.

◼ *The governing body*

Most countries have an organisation which oversees canoeing. In the UK this is the British Canoe Union (BCU). This is really your main resource: if the BCU can't give you direct help they will be able to put you in touch with someone who can. Joining the BCU gives you a good magazine, insurance, a waterways licence and other benefits. It represents canoeists in the serious matter of access to water in Britain. You can get a list of canoe clubs and regional coaching organisers from the BCU which will help you make contact with local paddlers.

The BCU operates a coaching scheme which runs courses in paddling skills. There is also an award scheme for training and approval of instructors at various levels.

▧ Books

There are a number of good books covering the more specialist aspects of canoeing with sea kayaking particularly well represented. There is also an increasing number of narrative books covering journeys by paddlers. The book which gives the most comprehensive coverage of the different aspects of canoeing is the *BCU Canoeing Handbook*. This contains most of the technical information needed to understand the sport and as such would be a good resource book. The canoeing magazines sell (via mail order) virtually all of the canoeing titles available in the UK.

▧ Magazines

There is only a small number of magazines serving canoeing but they do provide all the material you might expect from a sports periodical. Reading the magazines is the way quickly to get an idea of equipment prices and new developments in gear. All the big retailers and manufacturers advertise in them and there are private sales, results, event calendars as well as articles by paddlers. I would say that getting hold of a canoeing magazine would be an important early stage in getting your own paddling off the ground.

▧ Videos/films

Paddling kayaks and canoes is a visually striking sport and luckily plenty of people have taken the trouble to film it. There is lots of film and video material around and even film dating back to the early seventies is well worth viewing. A selection of instructional videos is available. These are definitely useful when you are teaching yourself, especially if you are short of other paddlers to see in action. An address of a canoe video retailer/hirer is on p. 169.

▧ Guidebooks/maps

Inland touring is reasonably well documented, especially where there is white water involved. Notable regions such as Snowdonia, Cumbria and the Highlands of Scotland are very well covered. Sea canoeing areas are much less written about, with the exception of North Wales, but the situation is improving every year. A full list of maps and guidebooks is given on the book trading pages of the magazines.

◪ *International Canoe Exhibition*

The International Exhibition is held each year and it really is the single event to attend if you want to see what the canoeing world is all about. The centrepiece is the display by manufacturers of boats and equipment and there are plenty of retailers around if you want to purchase. The exhibition is currently held at Crystal Palace where the swimming pool is used constantly for polo matches, demonstrations of boats and various specially prepared paddling contests. Videos and slide lectures are also on the programme.

The Canoe Exhibition usually takes place on a weekend in February.

◪ *National venues*

In the UK there are several places which have been set up very much to serve the sport. The National Watersports Centre at Holme Pierrepont, Nottingham is the best example. Here is a man-made white water/slalom course which runs constantly. There are always paddlers playing and training on the course and apart from at specific competition times the course is available to all. At the same site is a flatwater regatta course which is used for sprint racing events.

In North Wales is the National Water Centre on the river Tryweryn, just outside Bala. This is a dam-controlled river which offers the same kind of action as Nottingham in a more rural setting.

In other parts of the country there are regular events, usually in the form of competitions, where paddlers congregate. These are announced in the magazines' calendar sections.

—————— **Useful addresses** ——————

The British Canoe Union

Dudderidge House
Adbolton Lane
West Bridgford
Nottingham
NG2 5AS
Tel: (0602) 821100

Canoe Association of Northern Ireland

c/o Sports Council for Northern Ireland
House of Sport
Upper Malone Road
Belfast
BT9 5LA
Tel: (0232) 381222

Scottish Canoe Association

Caledonia House
South Gyle
Edinburgh
EH12 9DQ
Tel: (031) 317 7314

Welsh Canoe Association

Pen y Bont
Corwen
Clwyd
LL21 0EL
Tel: (0490) 2345

Irish Canoe Union

4/5 Eustace Street
Dublin 2
Ireland

International Federations

Australia

Australian Canoe Federation
Room 510
Sports House
157 Gloucester Street
Sydney
NSW 2000
Australia

Canada

Canadian Canoe Association
333 River Road
Vanier City
Ontario
K1L 8b9
Canada

France

Fédération Française de Canoe Kayak
17 Route de Vienne
69007 Lyon
France

Germany

Deutscher Kanu-Verband
Berta-allee 8
4100 Duisberg 1
Germany

New Zealand

New Zealand Canoe Association
PO Box 3768
Wellington
New Zealand

USA

American Canoe Association
8580 Cinderbed Road
Suite 1900
Newington
Virginia
USA

Magazines

Canoeist
4 Sinodun Row
Appleford
Oxon
OX14 4PE

Canoe Focus
See British Canoe Union

Videos/films

Chrisfilm and Video Ltd
The Mill Glasshouses
Pateley Bridge
Harrogate
North Yorks
NG3 5QH

Guidebooks/maps/touring information

International Long River Canoeist Club
Catalina Cottage
Aultvullin
Strathay Point
Sutherland
KW14 7RY

British Waterways
Melbury House
Melbury Terrace
London
NW1 6JX

Advanced Sea Kayak Club
7 Miller Close
Newport
Isle of Wight
PO30 5PS

Cordee
3a De Monfort Street
Leicester
LE1 7HD

DIY equipment/materials

Tor
3 Fryer Street
Runcorn
WA7 1ND

Pennine Outdoor
Hardknott
Holmbridge
Huddersfield
West Yorks

Resource books

British Canoe Union Members Yearbook

This book contains the following information:

- List of all BCU leaflets
- Information on National White Water Centres
- Dates of inland and international river tours
- List of access officers
- Suppliers of canoeing equipment
- Complete calendars for the year for marathon racing, slalom, polo, sailing, surf and wild water racing.
- List of tests and awards
- Calendar for the year of coaching courses
- Plus other useful items

The yearbook is free to members

The Outdoor Source Book
An excellent yearly publication full of useful information on outdoor courses and resources, available from Outdoor Education, Charlotte Mason College, Ambleside, Cumbria, LA22 9BB.

EAR

For information on Expired Air Resuscitation and Drowning:
Royal Lifesaving Society
Mountbatten House
Studley
Warwickshire B8O 7NN.

—————APPENDIX—————

Dealing with a person who appears to have drowned

CHECK FOR CONSCIOUSNESS AND BREATHING

Check for breathing by

- Looking for chest movement
- Listening at the mouth and feeling for air movement

IF BREATHING
- Place in recovery position
- Hospitalise
- Keep warm

IF NOT BREATHING
- Turn casualty onto back
- Obtain a clear airway
- If no response begin EAR
- Get someone to summon medical aid

DURING EAR
- Check for a pulse
- If none, commence Cardio Pulmonary Resuscitation (CPR)
- Keep going for as long as you are able or until a doctor says stop
- If the casualty revives, place in the recovery position

The safety record for people involved in canoeing is extremely good and serious accidents are rare. The facts show that recreational drowning accidents more frequently happen to people who have a once-only dabble at boating rather than a serious interest. In my experience canoeing makes you more respectful of water – not frightened but more acutely aware of the dangers and, importantly, how to behave in a way which reduces the danger almost entirely.

Expired Air Resuscitation

If, during your paddling, you come across a person whom you suspect has drowned you can, as a non-medical person, provide first aid treatment which may revive them. This action is called **Expired Air Resuscitation** (EAR). To be effective with EAR you need to act swiftly once you have found the casualty: you need to have practised it in a training context and you need to understand the simple, essential steps involved. No book can make you skilful in EAR. Only proper hands-on training such as you would get from a first-aid or life-saving organisation can do that.

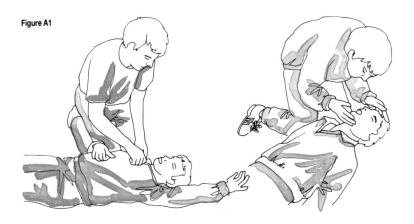

Figure A1

1 With the casualty on his back, remove any debris from his mouth and loosen tight clothing around his neck. Further clear the airway by lifting slightly under the neck and tilting the head backwards. Finally lift the chin upwards by pinching it with your thumb and forefinger.

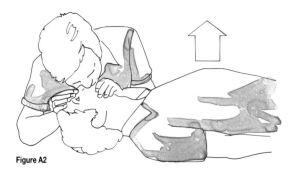

Figure A2

2   Pinch the casualty's nose. Take one full breath and make a seal over the open mouth with your own mouth. Breathe steadily into the casualty and watch for his chest rising. Give four of these breaths, taking your mouth away at the end of each.

If there is no revival, check for a pulse (at the side of the neck, in line with the Adam's apple). If there is no pulse you must start external chest compression to assist the heart beat and also keep up the EAR. This is called Cardio Pulmonary Resuscitaton (CPR).

Figure A3

Cardio Pulmonary Resuscitation

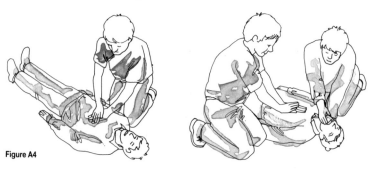

Figure A4

Work on a firm, flat surface. Feel for the front of the casualty's ribcage and find the breast bone (a long smooth bone running centrally down the chest). Place the heel of one hand on the centre of the lower half of the breast bone. With the other hand on top of this, interlock your fingers and with straight arms depress the breast bone about 4 cm (1½ inches) and then release.

Give 15 compressions at the rate of one per second. Two breaths of EAR may now be given and then return immediately to chest compressions. Continue with this ratio of 15 compressions to 2 breaths.

If you can get help with the work let one person do the compressions and the other the EAR. A ratio of 5 compressions to 1 breath is now possible.

Always use firm, vertical pressure for the compressions – violent or erratic action can be dangerous. Ensure that the casualty's airway is kept clear (head tilted back) at all times.

The recovery position

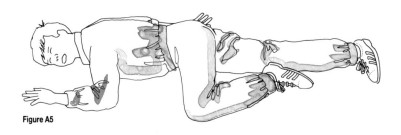

Figure A5

Any unconscious or revived person should be placed in the recovery position. It ensures that breathing remains unobstructed and yet can be observed closely. An unconscious or revived person should not be left on their back.

In the recovery position the upper arm and thigh on the same side are placed at right angles to the body. The opposite arm is straight and by the side.

NEVER LEAVE A REVIVED PERSON ALONE – BREATHING MIGHT STOP AGAIN. THEY ABSOLUTELY MUST BE HOSPI-TALISED.

INDEX

There are many more titles available in the Teach Yourself series. We give details of a few of them on the following pages. If you would like a catalogue listing all the titles in the series please write to the:

Marketing Executive, Teach Yourself Books
Hodder & Stoughton Publishers
Mill Road
Dunton Green
Sevenoaks
Kent TN13 2YA
England

TEACH YOURSELF
WALKING AND RAMBLING
HEATHER MACDERMID

Walking and Rambling is for anyone who wants to walk
in the country. It answers the questions which interest,
worry or intrigue walkers and gives plenty of practical
advice. Heather MacDermid is an experienced walker who
has introduced many people to country walking through
her local classes.

She introduces you to:

- planning your route
- using maps and guides
- your rights of way
- deciding how far to go and how long it will take
- forecasting the weather
- taking the right equipment
- dealing with bulls and other beasts
- finding your way
- walking with children
- walking alone or with companions
- leading a walk

and there is a major section describing some of the most
popular paths in Britain.

ISBN 0340 567791

TEACH YOURSELF
GOLF
RYDER CUP CAPTAIN BERNARD GALLACHER
AND MARK WILSON

All golfers, from junior novice to superstar professional,
are united by one indisputable attraction: there is no end
to the process of learning to play the game.

Teach Yourself Golf has been written and illustrated to
meet the needs of golfers of all standards. It covers every
department of the game, from choosing a set of clubs to
detailed advice on how to play the trouble shots that win
competitions. The language of golf for those who play and
those who follow the game through televised tournaments
is explained in a comprehensive glossary.

Whatever your handicap or experience, this book will help
you learn, improve and enjoy the game more than ever.

*'A book which could make a big impact for the beginner and
the novice.'*   Golf Illustrated

ISBN 0340 561483

TEACH YOURSELF
BADMINTON
ALLAN CAMPBELL

The fast-growing sport of badminton can be enjoyed at all levels and by all ages. Beginners and experienced players alike will find this guide an invaluable source of advice and hints on how to improve their game.

This book begins with advice on choosing equipment and getting started. It goes on to give in-depth tuition on the various strokes, including net play and serving, and tactics for all types of game. A section is also included on fitness for badminton.

ISBN 0340 523743

TEACH YOURSELF
KARATE
STEVE ARNEIL AND LIAM KEAVENEY

Karate is one of the most effective forms of unarmed self-defence. Its popularity with people of all ages stems not only from this, but also from the feeling of mental and physical confidence that training in Karate brings.

Teach Yourself Karate is a complete introductory course for beginners, but it is also an ideal refresher course for those who already know the basics. If you want to master Karate on your own, or just practise outside your *dojo*, this is the book for you.

Highly-illustrated throughout, it includes:

- the basic principles for success
- clubs and club etiquette
- exercise for fitness and stamina
- stances
- blocks
- punching and striking
- kicking
- fighting and sparring
- combination techniques
- *kata*
- tournaments
- self-defence
- Japanese names, with complete explanations in English

Between them, Steve Arneil and Liam Keaveney have been involved in the martial arts for 60 years. Steve Arneil (7th Dan) is Chief Instructor of the British Karate Kyokushinkai and Chairman of the European Kyokushin Organisation. Liam Keaveney (3rd Dan) is Head Representative of the Irish Karate Kyokushin Organisation and Secretary of the European Kyokushin Organisation.

ISBN 0340 52782X